The Apostolic Conciliarism of
Jean Gerson

AAR

The American Academy of Religion
The Religions

Editor
Paul B. Courtright

Number 4

THE APOSTOLIC CONCILIARISM OF JEAN GERSON

John J. Ryan

The Apostolic Conciliarism of
Jean Gerson

JOHN J. RYAN

Scholars Press
Atlanta

THE APOSTOLIC CONCILIARISM OF JEAN GERSON

Copyright © 1998 by the American Academy of Religion

All Rights Reserved.

No part of this work may be reproduced or transmitted in any form or by any means, electronic or mechanical, including photocopying and recording, or by means of any information storage or retrieval system, except as may be expressly permitted by the 1976 Copyright Act or in writing from the publisher. Requests for permission should be addressed in writing to the Rights and Permissions Department, Scholars Press, P.O. Box 15399, Atlanta, GA 30333-0399, USA.

Library of Congress Cataloging-in-Publication Data

Ryan, John J. (John Joseph), 1925 —
    The apostolic conciliarism of Jean Gerson / John J. Ryan.
        p.   cm. — (AAR the religions; no. 4)
    Includes bibliographical references.
    ISBN 0-7885-0464-9 (pbk. : alk. paper)
    1. Gerson, Jean, 1363–1429 — Contributions in conciliar theory.
2. Conciliar theory — History of doctrines — Middle Ages, 600–1500.
I. Title. II. Series.
BV720.R93 1998
262'.02'092 — dc21   98-21363
                                                                                      CIP

This book is printed on recycled, acid-free paper.

98 99 00 01 02 03 04 05 06 07 — 10 9 8 7 6 5 4 3 2 1

MANUFACTURED IN THE UNITED STATES OF AMERICA

Contents

Preface 7

Introduction 10

Chapter 1: Medieval Apostolic Protest 14

Chapter 2: The "Apostolic" Gerson 23

Chapter 3: Development 30

Chapter 4: Apostolic Notes 40

Chapter 5: The Church as Apostolic Council 64

Notes 79

Bibliography 92

Preface

Although the high Middle Ages experienced a full flourishing of the Church's canon law and its jurisprudence, not until the turn into the fourteenth century did the theology of the Church emerge as a specific theme for theologians. Even then this ecclesiology did not appear in a pure state but as a series of disparate questions suggested or provoked by current ecclesial developments and controversies, especially the then still-murky dispute between what somewhat later would be called "church and state." For the most part, except for Reformation controversies and their aftermath, it has since then led a mostly collateral existence, influenced as much by political controversy as by reform mentalities.

Since at least the work of J. N. Figgis, the skill and aptitude of late-medieval conciliar thinkers for political theory has engendered much praise and interest for their anticipation of modern representative and even democratic political theory. This turn of scholarship has been treated like a two-edged sword by Roman Catholic apologists, useful for encouraging a more receptive attitude toward Roman Catholic ideas about modern secular culture, while regarded as having one edge rather too sharp when wielded in questions of papal authority within the Roman church. Strict constructionists of papal ecclesiastical absolutism react to the trumpeting of conciliarism's "democratic" germs as indeed a back-handed compliment.

In the nineteenth century the Roman Catholic Church, enjoying a wide resurgence of popular interest and influence, tried to lay all of the most important questions of the theology of the Church to rest by the pronouncements of the First Vatican Council, whose work was never really finished. The religious movement called ecumenism, especially in the past several decades, has been forced to acknowledge that doctrinal matters can never be finally really resolved without a head-on confrontation with the questions about ecclesial authority as such, whether in doctrine, devotion, or organizational life as a whole.

Actually, ecumenism's early career was propelled not by doctrinal problems but more by considerations arising from the missionary endeavors of the churches. This was yet another case of practicalities and actualities outrunning theory. Even during the Reformation, the theology of the Church had been part of a confused mix of basic experiences of faith, fixing themselves in doctrinal obsessions and cultic phobias.

Current ecumenical efforts now have to face the most basic questions of religious faith: the exact nature and locus of any such thing as religious faith, and the idea and rationally defensible ground for any such thing as "revelation" in the religious sense encompassing all the great world religions. Only then can hopes for a successful, contemporaneously adequate enunciation of ideas of *authority* in matters of religious faith be realistic.

To return to the ecumenical efforts within Christianity itself, Heiko Oberman, especially, has lead the way in showing us the doctrinal seeds of the Reformation in the late-medieval Church, while Brian Tierney has done the same for medieval canonical developments revealing there the germination of late-medieval conciliarism. As Oberman has shown that the Reformation chose among live options, so a large implication of the work of Tierney and others is that some aspects of conciliar thought may now be live options for the churches, the Roman Catholic among them. Indeed, some of those orientations made an appearance during Vatican II, an appearance which was rather hesitant and, for all the rampant ballyhoo about them in Roman Catholic circles, quite tentative and timorous. The present effort to mine yet another vein of the conciliarist contribution is meant to contribute to these current explorations of medieval sources in the later Christian churches, not in the discussion of specific doctrinal or cultic issues, but in the very *idea* of Church and then, more immediately and practically, in the locus of Church *authority* in its vital functions.

Thus it should be clearly understood that this investigation is not formally a work of systematic, doctrinal, or constructive theology. It could be called theological only in the sense that it attempts to embody, as Gerson did, vital concerns of the Christian Sacred Scriptures; it is theology as that Scripture is theology. Indeed, those who have investigated the matter discovered some time ago that even as a philosopher-theologian, Gerson, expert at grasping the systems of others, is not really, across the whole range of his thought, a systematizer but something of an eclectic improviser, structuring his conceptions according to the needs of the object in view. Even his mystical writing, which gives throughout a clear grasp of system, is not an original conception but largely taken from his sources. In Gerson's conciliar thought, in particular, all talk of system is out of place.

Conciliar thought as such, this study seeks to imply, is still a live option for the churches. It is so because, it will here be claimed, its core realizations are apostolic. The Christian churches will continue to be vital to the religious flourishing of human culture only to the extent that they remain and develop as apostolic.

This work is intended as an inquiry in intellectual history, and specifically the conciliar thought of only one of the conciliarists—although the most influential of them all, who in his own work sums up almost all the most prevalent emphases of the last great medieval surge of conciliar thought. Such a description is the special distinction of Jean Charlier de Gerson, the one-time chancellor of the University of Paris, the Church's leading theological institution of that age. The author is quite conscious of the fact that this work is only a beginning of a much larger task for himself and for others, pursuing a path opened (for this researcher) by the work and example of Scott Hendrix, Tony Black, and Gordon Leff, a path which must be further traversed by others following the trail of apostolic concerns and echoes of the medieval apostolic disputes from the beginning of conciliar thought into the modern era.

It remains for me only to thank those so helpful to me, among whom should be especially mentioned Mr. Yves Gaudreau, for his handling of the practical matters which the author has always found beyond his distracted competence, and Prof. Charles Draimin of Concordia University, Montreal, for invaluable aid with business matters and all the emerging electronic challenges of this fantastic new world of written communication.

Introduction

If there is some point in observing that "nothing succeeds like success" then the obverse of the dictum also might be ventured: nothing fails like failure. A well-known axiom of historical research says that history tends to be the story of the winners. This provides the revisionist historian an always fertile field for excavating and reappraising the failures. But the story of late-medieval conciliarism exhibits a curious contradiction of this axiom. Seldom has so much been preserved and examined of the advocacy of so notable a historical failure. Indeed, seldom has so much commiseration been tendered through the years by sympathetic onlookers of the struggle (*not* Roman Catholic) along with praise for the creative effects of conciliar theory upon the development of modern constitutionalism.[1]

And yet no one seems to be in doubt about why such a praiseworthy effort failed. For Roman Catholics, of course (until the recent past), conciliarism failed because it was at root a heresy against the divine institution of strict papal monarchy, and all heresies must fall before the indefectibility of the Church. For non-Romans, the intellectual strength of conciliarism was also its weakness: what has constitutional theory to do with a Church founded on the Word of God? What has Aristotelian *epikeia* to do with saving faith? Conciliarism was, after all, a secularizing intrusion, a movement of opportunistic political strategy (however well-intentioned) into the spiritual sanctuary of Christian living. All too clearly the conciliarist had invoked legal theory, and by legal theory had misunderstood spiritual reality. And here those without religious interests would agree with the non-Roman judgment: this secular subversion met its ironically apt nemesis—the incorrigible authoritarianism of Rome.

INTRODUCTION

And hereby the conciliarists are misunderstood. Legal theory and the canon law of the Church may have been their chief strategic weapons; they were not their inspiration or motivation. Those lay elsewhere. Awakened from the "dogmatic slumber" of the high Middle Ages by the continuing dire peril of the Church, the conciliarists finally found their organizing motivation and inspiration in the tradition of apostolic protest. That, specifically in the case of Jean Charlier de Gerson, most important of the conciliarists, is the contention of this study.

The effort here will be to bring together into one focus two different currents of inquiry into medieval history not usually seen together. It will attempt to examine late-medieval conciliarism in the perspective of the medieval movements of "apostolic" protest. Both inquiries have experienced some rethinking in recent decades. Medieval "apostolic" protest is no longer generally seen in the light of what now appear to be its more extreme manifestations (e.g., the Catharists or the Free Spirit). These now are sometimes described as alien imports into the religious currents of the Middle Ages.[2] It begins to appear that reformist protest in the name of the original apostolic life was fermenting all across the Western Church and manifesting genuinely Christian concerns.[3]

Medieval conciliarism has likewise begun to emerge (for Roman Catholics) from the charge of heresy and (for other students of medieval life) from that of a politicizing and secularizing opportunism, an alien thing for church life.[4] Heiko Oberman observes that "the goals of conciliarism are not correctly understood when regarded as anti-papal." Its goals were rather, in words he cites from the contemporary Dietrich von Niem, "one undivided Church . . . and moral reform by return to the mores of the early church."[5] In Oberman's view the concern in conciliar research with the means of implementation for ending the schism has lead to a "deficit in attention given to the *aims* striven after" (Oberman, 31). Conciliarism can now be seen, even in Roman Catholic circles, against a background of traditional thinking within the Church, most importantly in the earlier ecclesiastical tradition of canon law.[6] Oberman notes the mention of "mores of the early church" by Niem. But it has been Gordon Leff, Antony Black, and Scott Hendrix who have most explicitly seen the confluence of these two currents, suggesting that conciliar thought has a vital root in this medieval "apostolic" protest.[7]

This study will attempt to expose that "vital root" and remedy the "attention deficit" by establishing and developing the conciliar aims in the thought of Jean Charlier de Gerson, perhaps conciliarism's most influential medieval spokesman. Specifically, the attempt will be to show that Gerson's reformism was clearly and strongly "apostolic" in the historic sense in which that word came to be understood during the Middle Ages.

Gerson's conciliar teachings are too well known and thoroughly canvassed to need rehearsing, except to show them against a historical and theological background which steadily grows richer and more complex.[8] Many elements of that background Gerson shares with the various apostolic movements which flourished in the decades framing his life's work. Research of recent decades has shown the extent of Gerson's ecclesiastical orthodoxy, his almost overdeveloped sense of the hierarchical and the clerical in the Church.[9] But this reclaiming of him for orthodox values can risk missing a special interest his ecclesiology holds for the contemporary situation. In this ecumenical age, demanding all sorts of mediations, doctrinal, ecclesiastical, and theological, it is opportune to note that Gerson has always been known as a mediating thinker.[10] We can add a new dimension to that mediation: Gerson attempted to mediate between official ecclesiastical life and the apostolic movements of the age by creating an *ecclesiastical version* of the medieval apostolic protest.

More clearly and comprehensively than any of his contemporaries, Gerson's reform efforts in general and his ecclesiological thinking in particular reveal a concern to purify and renew the Church's official life and pastoral practice by incorporating what he considered the authentic values in the long-standing programs of protest and renewal centering on the call to return to the "apostolic" life.[11] It is true that he is concerned enough to establish the orthodoxy of his own programs to go almost out of his way to condemn as excessive and even pernicious several features endemic in some forms of "apostolic" protest. But there can be no mistaking the substantial identity of his conception of Christian ecclesiastical life and the central values of the various apostolic movements. We will mark the emergence of his apostolic concerns and then examine their effects upon his program of Church reform, especially as these concerns eventuate in positions commonly regarded as conciliar.

Chapter 1

Medieval Apostolic Protest

The topography of medieval apostolic protest has in recent decades emerged in much greater detail, but the watershed remains the same: the era of the Gregorian Reform.[1] In his classic development of Max Weber's church-sect typology, Ernst Troeltsch looks forward to the Gregorian era from the start of the history of the Christian churches. He points to the fact that from the beginning there was, along with the social development of the early church, a world-indifferent radicalism which was evoked by the worldly compromise of the Church and which "broke forth afresh with extraordinary power" in the central period of the Middle Ages [i.e., the beginning of the Gregorian era].[2] Its first important social manifestation was, paradoxically, an institutional one, the appearance at Rome of a new, reforming papacy, one officially intent upon restoring primitive purity.[3] The unmistakeably "monastic" coloration of this reform embraced the idea that "all the apostles were truly monks" and appears to have been impressed by the monastic renewals typified by the founding of Cluny in Burgundy in 910, which Morris calls "the first attempt to embody the apostolic ideal in a new organization" (Morris, 136). This is not to say that the apostolic ideal was new to monasticism. As Hendrix points out, the apostolic ideal had been invoked throughout the centuries of monasticism.[4] Hildebrand himself in the Synod of Rome (1059) urged the monastic style of communal living without personal property upon the parish clergy (Hendrix, 138), thereby launching the canonical life for clergy which was not long in receiving an apostolic interpretation. Indeed, Anselm of Havelberg inverts the traditional ranking of monks over clerics by stating his opinion that clerics are higher than monks because they live both active and contemplative lives, like Christ, and are thus the true *vita apostolica*.[5] Such is also the opinion of Rupert of Deutz, who titles his work *De vita vere apostolica*.[6]

But the Gregorian reform impulse could scarcely be confined to monasticism and the rule for canons. The apostolic renewal also broke out among the laity, finding its expression in efforts toward self-conquest and brotherly love.[7]

At this point a clear distinction must be drawn between these movements of apostolic renewal and the so-called "Apostolics," the Joachimite offshoot of penitentials formed by a certain Gerard Segarelli of Parma in 1260, who originated the first flagellant processions and whose apocalypticism was regarded as heretical from the outset.[8] As Gordon Leff has emphasized, such heretical movements were rare and atypical of apostolic reform.[9]

It is true, of course, that initially the Church could tolerate such unaccustomed ideas only in the form of monasticism, so that these ideals were forced to find a development alongside of the Church, and produced the new type of the sect (Troeltsch, 1:330–32). Troeltsch described the latter as taking the Sermon on the Mount as its ideal, practicing renunciation "only as a means of charity, as the basis of a thorough-going communism of love" (Troeltsch, 1:332). He thought that the sect idea had disappeared with the Donatist African Christianity and only reappeared in a decisive form after "the completion of the idea of the Church" in the Gregorian reform (Troeltsch, 1:333). In constructing their alternatives to the corruption of the Church, the sects always started from the teaching and example of Jesus, "from the subjective work of the apostles and the pattern of their lives of poverty" (Troeltsch, 1:342). Among the characteristic features of the sects he noted, among others, "religious equality and brotherly love . . . [and] the separation of the religious life from the economic struggle by means of the ideal of poverty and frugality" (Troeltsch, 1:336). There is an echo of this view of medieval apostolic activity as sectarian in Francis Oakley's remark that the ecclesiastical reforms of the Gregorian age "sponsored a revival of the Donatist vision of a church of the pure, the essentially sectarian vision of a church composed exclusively of the committed and the saintly."[10] But recent research in the main, hesitating before the extremist connotations of the idea of sect, has shown that this ferment in the Middle Ages had originally an orthodox origin and continued to have orthodox expressions well into the twelfth century.[11]

The research of Gerhart Ladner has shown that the concepts of reform and renewal are specifically Christian, arising from Christian views of the significance of temporal life and the return to original forms. The "Church of the Apostles" is the ideal in every Christian Age, which Ladner traces through the patristic era.[12] M.-D. Chenu, describing apostolic reform and renewal in the twelfth century, points to the shift away from monasticism as the ideal of the apostolic life.[13] Colin Morris notes the appearance at the beginning of the twelfth century of numerous hermits in Flanders and Northern France,[14] Henry Mayr-Harting remarking in the same work that a proliferation of hermits tends to occur "when Christian society perceives a gap between ecclesiastical and spiritual power." That gap had opened because of the eleventh-century reform movement (Mayr-Harting, 115).

But this popular movement found itself checked, according to Morris, by "the juridicalization of the Church from the middle of the twelfth century" (Morris, 139). Ironically, it was the influence of that same Gregorian reform that now attempted to preempt the apostolic spirit for the institutional Church and the immensely strengthened prestige of the papacy. The ultimate failure of this institutional impulse, Oakley observes, actually extended the apostolic vision and led to "the emergence of an underground [not necessarily heterodox] current of opposition to official ecclesiastical pretensions."[15] This new current was apparently spearheaded by the hermits of northern France. One of them, Stephen of Muret, issued a new battle cry: "No Rule except the Gospel of Christ." Morris describes what ensued:

> On this interpretation, the apostolic life could be opened to ordinary people, either by accepting them directly into communities or by creating communities of preachers and ministers who would live in their midst. A 'poverty and preaching' tradition arose, most notably in France. (Morris, 139)

From the time of its clear emergence in the mid-eleventh century, apostolic protest had sought to purify even the "apostolic" life of monasticism of worldly wealth and indulgence. The great and fierce St. Bernard, most famous of early-twelfth-century monastic reformers, has left this memorable comment:

> The walls of the [monastic] church are indeed resplendent, but her poor go needy. She clothes her stones with gold and leaves her children to go naked. The eyes of the rich are flattered at the expense of the poor. The delicate find the wherewithal to gratify their taste, but the miserable find nothing to satisfy hunger.[16]

But early in the twelfth century, interest apparently began to develop elsewhere. These movements had come to focus on clerical wealth and power as the chief ills of the Christian life, with material poverty and itinerant preaching as the key remedies. Such new expressions of protest and renewal are not easy to categorize. Constable refers to the "new and anomalous types of religious life" springing up in the twelfth century all over Europe—lay penitents, "worshippers of God," men and women, lay confraternities (Constable, 35–36). The center of apostolic protest was now the life of the developing towns of the twelfth century.[17] Leff has emphasized that with the exception of the Cathars and the Free Spirits, these groups began in authentically Christian inspiration, moving only through rejection and isolation into heterodoxy.[18]

The preaching carried on in France by wandering hermits sometimes resulted in the foundation of orthodox religious congregations,[19] but the spreading enthusiasm reveals some interesting new strands in popular piety. Lambert tells us of a diffused reverence for extreme asceticism and poverty. Poverty and preaching were closely linked and speedily attracted followers, mixed bodies of men and women who attached themselves to the preachers as they travelled round the countryside (Lambert, 44–45).[20] Their contemporaries recognized the model they were striving to emulate. "It is striking how the sources, both for heretical movements and for the wandering preachers, speak of the apostolic life as a mark of these spontaneous phenomena" (Lambert, 46).

But this is no longer the monastic understanding of apostolic life according to the pattern of the early Christians at Jerusalem.

A new understanding was emerging, based on the texts of Matthew and Luke about Christ sending out the Seventy to wander preaching through the villages, having neither scrip nor purse nor shoes and taking no money with them (Lambert, 46).[21] But Lambert points out that this more modern view of the apostolic life was encouraged by an accumulation of influences, by the reforms of the canonical life (from the last quarter of the eleventh century),[22] by a reaction against the developing bourgeoisie, and also by an increasing "popular rationalism, capable in a groping way of making comparisons with a new historical sense between the simple Church of the Apostles and the elaborate hierarchical Church of the twelfth century" (Lambert, 46). This "new historical sense" is also marked by Leff, who explains that "the Bible in being used historically made Christ an historical figure. His life and words . . . became a challenge to the life and practices of the present church."[23]

Eventually these lay apostolic groups, with a popular preacher at their center, sometimes himself a layman (like Peter Waldo and his "poor men of Lyons"),[24] began to be recruited among university students and town artisans. At the same time plenty of humble people, both men and women, were busy studying and teaching the Word of God. Their sincere efforts to equip themselves for this work show their commitment to it, as is evidenced by the study of writings, handbooks, translations, by which they prepared themselves for the task of evangelization. Such evangelical knowledge yielded remarkable initiatives and gave ordinary men and women "an active share in the ministry of the Word."[25]

In the story of the rise of the Beguines and the history of Mary of Oignes, we find James of Vitry travelling in southern France in the first third of the thirteenth century and becoming aware of "the international dimensions of what was happening: everywhere there were pious confraternities arising, inspired by apostolic ideals." The impetus was primarily urban and recruiting was mainly among women of the propertied classes,[26] but James specifies "clerics, priests, married people, widows, virgins, soldiers, merchants, peasants, craftsmen, and 'other multiform types of men.'"[27] The social ferment seems to have been general.

All this apostolic activity was the obverse of the continuing protest, the overarching theme of which is the betrayal by the institutional Church, specifically its clergy, of the primitive apostolic community as testified to in Scripture. That testimony in the first place is to a *fraternal* life thought of as spiritual, poor, and simple, as practiced by Christ and the Apostles, devoted to the itinerant preaching of the Word and fraternal love practiced in a common life among those personally dispossessed (ideally) of all material goods. The twin enabling conditions of this life are preaching and faith, the conditions which give living power to the Word of Scripture. The first effects of preaching and the faith which responds to it ought to be, it was thought, a common life of love and shared poverty (Acts 4:32).

But it would be easy to adopt an excessively schematic, detailed conception of this apostolic protest, as though it were a clearly articulated and uniform program (somewhat as the institutional Church has always looked upon the heresies which challenged it). It is far more likely to have been in any one example sketchy and not too coherent. Probably no two groups had exactly the same view of what the apostolic life actually involved. But these seem to have been the recurring themes, the "marks" of the apostolic view of the Church: Scripture, preaching, faith, community, poverty, service. None, of course, is a new emphasis; the distinctiveness of the apostolics' appropriation of them is their sense of a profound connection among these "marks"—Scripture as a call to action, involving preaching; preaching as a demand for obedience involving faith and service; faith and service as a summons to community and to an unworldly poverty; and so on. Some form of these interconnections was in a multitude of differing ways erected as a prophetic norm for criticism of and judgment upon the contemporary Church and as a program for renewal.[28]

Throughout the high Middle Ages the protest movements manifest a clearly recognizable consistency and continuity, their changing forms and fortunes responding to the perceived ills of the institutional Church. The growth in the temporal power and prestige of the later-twelfth-century papacy cost it the loss in leadership of popular religious sentiment, which then tended, as has been noted above, to flow out of the Church into marginal or heretical sects rather than, as earlier, into new religious houses

(Lambert, 84). Throughout the fourteenth century, with the loss of vitality of the major religious orders, "a popular religion blossomed in the towns, in the parish churches, and in the confraternities," with a great vogue for popular devotions in the vernacular and the dissemination of scriptural compilations. Preachers, often now from the regular clergy, readily drew to the churches large crowds of laity more impatient of clerical deficiencies now that they were better educated, with "widening horizons . . . and an increasing lay self-consciousness and independence" (Lambert, 210).

This ferment is the historical context of what is, of course, the central chapter in the story of medieval apostolic reforms: the phenomenon of Francis of Assisi and his "Little Brothers," who early in the thirteenth century captivated even the papacy and in succeeding decades took the devotional life of the common people almost by storm. Their ideal of the true apostolic life was characterized, in a way singular among approved religious orders, by the emphasis upon total poverty in imitation of the poverty of Christ and the Apostles and the daily practice of begging.[29] The saga of the Minorites is an epitome of the progress of many earlier movements of apostolic reform, beginning with a papally approved form of religious life and poverty to an internal dissension which early in the fourteenth century saw some of the most devoted and idealistic Franciscans condemned by Pope John XXII for their unyielding insistence upon a radical doctrine of the absolute poverty of Christ and the Apostles.[30] The several papal bulls involved in this condemnation so alarmed official circles in the Church that any further efforts to institutionalize the apostolic life were greeted with overwhelming resistance.

Nevertheless, further evidence shows that the popular ferment did not die. Gerald Strauss finds typical concerns of the apostolic movement clearly in evidence on the eve of the Reformation in the protests of all classes of German society.[31] Glenn Olsen notes that almost every sense of the idea of the primitive Church developed in the eleventh and twelfth centuries and recorded in the canonists still existed in the fifteenth century.[32] Gordon Leff thus must have something more particular in mind in considering the reemergence of the ideal of an "apostolic"

Church as "the great new ecclesiological fact of the later Middle Ages."[33] For the "great new fact" was ecclesiological in the broad sense. "From the later thirteenth century until the Reformation, the significant area of development in the religious life was found not in the formally patented religious orders but in the various group manifestations of lay piety."[34] Margaret Aston explains that "the renewal of the Church, the call to evangelical regeneration . . . was expressed in this period [the fourteenth and fifteenth centuries] from below." Ordinary believers found for themselves a spiritual independence remote from the ecclesiastical hierarchy.[35]

But even before the Franciscan poverty controversy had erupted, late in the thirteenth century the Church's moral authority and temporal power had begun to seem to many a thoughtful observer highly questionable. Hendrix says that at that point the concept of the apostolic life was joined to a new questioning of the structure and authority of the hierarchical Church.[36] At that point, one might add, the heretofore sectarian appeal to the apostolic life sounded clearly within Church circles and among its learned.

Now for the first time in the orthodox theological world, ecclesiastical and especially papal power became a subject for controversy, and the first treatises on ecclesiology appeared in the early fourteenth century.[37] Significantly, Leff notes (justly, if with less than abundant evidence) that John of Paris, one of the two to publish the earliest of these ecclesiological treatises, "arrived at a modified doctrine of the apostolic ideal."[38] Soon after, with the writings of Marsilius and William of Ockham, the idea of the general council made its appearance, not as the organ of papal centralism, as heretofore, but precisely as a challenge to it. Marsilius published in his *Defensor pacis* what may have been the first of the historically and theologically learned treatises which "took the primitive church as the model for what the present church should be. . . . Christ and his apostles had lived in poverty, simplicity, and equality."[39] Marsilius called for the control and, if need be, the correction of the papacy by a general council,[40] but his conception of the council was so secularized that it could scarcely offer a realistic current reform appeal. It was Ockham, who in his *Dialogus* spoke of the council (somewhat) as currently conceived, who set forth the first historically consequential suggestion of a council to reform the papacy. Ockham had, of course, not envisioned precisely the circumstances which now confronted the late-fourteenth-century Church, but R. Baumer says that for the first time "reform" and "council" are "almost equivalent."[41] It is thus not surprising that among other proposals advanced to solve the crisis of the double papal election of 1378 there early emerged a call for a general council. To this developing discussion, besides some antagonists in both papal curias and their political allies, there was an important contribution from the universities and their theologians, first of all from the "establishment" faculty at the University of Paris. Henry of Langenstein of the university wrote his *Epistola pacis* in 1379, while later that same year Conrad of Gelnhausen published his *Epistola brevis*.[42]

Chapter 2

The "Apostolic" Gerson

Jean Gerson, as a newly minted university theologian at Paris, had (besides his mentor, Pierre D'Ailly[1]) almost a generation of theological discussion of the problem of ecclesiastical and especially papal power on which to draw. He incorporated into the general discussion of the problem his own conception of reform, in which we can now recognize what has historically come to be called apostolic protest. His version is, of course, that of a schooled theologian and a Churchman of instinctively mediating tendencies.[2] If in comparison with the violence of sectarian diatribes Gerson's prophetic fervor seems less categorical and has nothing of the "slash-and-burn" about it, it must be said that what he wanted above all was a genuinely *ecclesiastical* expression of apostolic values, acknowledging the Church's venerable traditions and forms, renewing their original spirit (as he saw it). It is the purpose of this study to show that his concern for these values led him to conciliarism as surely as did the contemporary situation.

The Paris chancellor did not begin his career as an upholder of conciliar theory.[3] His first conciliarist proposals (1408–09) have a prehistory of only a half dozen or so years of published theoretical moves made in that direction. Indeed, seen from the perspective of his apostolic-reformist mentality, there is something misleading about treating Gerson as a conciliarist *tout court*. Conciliarist he certainly became, one of the most famous and influential in the movement in its critical early-fifteenth-century phase, which produced the events of Pisa and Constance. But, as we shall see, Gerson turned to conciliarism late in his career and then largely out of desperation, after finding that all the more conventional efforts to solve the papal schism had failed. At this point his reformist impulsion towards apostolic renewal led him to decide that the unrealized pursuit of unity lay ineluctably down the path of conciliarist strategy. At this point, sometime in 1408–09, he appears to have seized upon conciliarist principles which had long been familiar to him from the troubled debates of his time. Until then these ideas had been only implicit as one outcome of his apostolic ideals. Now he appears to have decided that unity demanded a conciliar solution, most particularly that the Church has an inherent right where necessary to assemble itself in council, whether or not the pope or any papal claimant is willing.

But it is the contention of this study that the ultimate understanding or conception of the reality of Church which drives *his* conciliar thinking (not to speak of anyone else's) *cannot* be enunciated in political or legal or philosophical or mystical categories. *His* reality of the Church is simpler and more primal than these: it is the vision of the Church *as an apostolic gathering*, an "ecumenical council by divine convocation," as Hans Küng has called it.[4]

In this perspective it is disappointing to read so eminent a scholar of the history of canon law and medieval political theory (as well as their conciliarist outcomes) as Brian Tierney still attempting to fit Gerson's conciliarism into some of the discussions he conducts in his article "Conciliarism, Corporatism, and Individualism: The Doctrine of Individual Rights in Gerson."[5] There we find Gerson's conciliarism explained in terms of a "doctrine of rights," amid the alternatives of a "corporatist" and an "individualist" [political] ideology. Certainly Gerson can be discussed in these categories. An erudite academician, he was familiar not only with his ecclesiastical lore of theology, philosophy, canon law, and church history, but also with legal and political theory. He was never slow to utilize any of this in support of his reform aims, and few are as competent to discuss the legal and political aspects of his thinking as is Tierney. The latter quite properly sees this side of his theoretical learning and reflection entering into his conciliar and theological writing in many important concerns. And Tierney understands as well as anyone Gerson's reformist aims, his deep concern for spirituality, and the spiritual welfare of the individual soul. But he is at least incautious in suggesting that concerns of political or legal theory are at the heart of Gerson's *conciliar* vision. When he talks about conciliar thinkers [and by implication Gerson] "adapting the scriptural doctrine to their own purposes by reformulating it in juridical or political language" (p. 83), perhaps one might suggest that the "scriptural doctrine" is closer to Gerson's "own purposes" than is the "juridical or political language."

Tierney's approach has a persistent tendency to treat Gerson's scriptural citations as "imagery" in pursuit of some legal theory he is really after. Might it not be that the legal theory is only a corollary, a translation of the ecclesial reality pointed to by the scripture? Tierney argues that "the context of medieval conciliarism is the truly significant one" for Gerson's theory of rights. That perhaps should be granted. But then to include, as Tierney proceeds to do (p. 93ff.), all of Gerson's reformist vision as comprised in *conciliarist* goals amounts to mistaking a means for an end, missing his ultimate apostolic vision. Louis Pascoe is much nearer to the heart of the matter in his reading of Gerson's pseudo-Dionysian understanding of the nature of the Church and his Bernardine mysticism.[6] But even that approach is too particularized and schematic to catch the originating impulse of the Gersonian ecclesiology.

It is the contention of this study that the rich contributions of historical research into the development of canon law and of medieval political theory and constitutionalism in the work of Ullmann, Tierney, Oakley, and others have done about as much as they can at present in illuminating the conciliar thinking of Gerson. The suggestions of Leff, Hendricks, and Black about sources closer to the wellsprings of theology and religious renewal must now be pursued.

From the outset of his ecclesiastical work, Gerson evinced concerns and values which place him in the tradition of the "apostolic" reformers. This early and abiding temper has at least as much to do with his subsequent conciliarism as the development of events. In this sense his career is again a lesson that conciliarism was not significantly the pragmatic *ad hoc* response to a situation of impasse, the bastard offspring of ecclesiastical misadventure. Rather it was an organic, reformist response to the *cul de sac* of the ecclesiastical situation. Indeed the connection of events with both reformism and conciliarism is clearly discernible in Gerson's development. As the conciliarist temperature rises in his work one notices much more frequent and emphatic "apostolic" utterances. Through the pressure of events the apostolic temper appears to issue in more and more explicit conciliarist claims. Both apostolic and conciliarist temperatures are at their highest reading, as one might expect, at the Council of Constance. In the course of this development one can see Gerson move from a relatively tranquil pursuit of apostolic goals by means of normal Church functioning to a final theory which strains to conceive apostolic community as realizable only through the Church's latent virtualities, not its ordinary processes.

Our earliest genuine Gerson text appears to be the Epiphany sermon preached on January 6, 1391, before the king and princes of the blood.[7] The atmosphere at that time in the course of the schism was one of hope. On November 9, 1389, a new pope, Boniface IX, had succeeded Urban VI at Rome, and shortly thereafter talks had been scheduled between him and his Avignonese rival. Everyone hoped to see peace and the end of the schism, with the university of Paris making insistent representations to the king in this vein, while the king himself was still contemplating the *via facti* (the use of force).[8] The purpose of the sermon appears to have been twofold: to move the king to act to end the schism and to induce him to lift a recent ban on public discussion of the schism in the university. In it Gerson paints a black picture of the situation: "Behold a Church lost, a Faith collapsed, and Christianity fallen . . ." (*Oeuvres*, d. 219, 5:36).

The tone and diction are deliberately evocative of Biblical prophecy and launch his career as an "apostolic" reformer. Already in this sermon as well, he expresses the conciliarist idea that even the papacy must be subordinated to the welfare of the Church as a whole. "It would be intolerable that this [i.e., the papacy] which was instituted for the good of the Church should turn to the Church's grave damage" (*Oeuvres*, d. 219, 5:38). But as subsequent events would show, Gerson contemplates no action without the pope, whom he at the time is one with the French Church as a whole in regarding as the Avignonese claimant, Clement VII. The position he takes here is not a conciliarist one: it will be years before he will consider a council even possible, much less obligatory. But here at the outset he holds the "apostolic" view that the ultimate good of the Church—its "charity"—is separable from any office or law. No orthodox theologian before the age of schism could have admitted this (unless in this matter Ockham is to be regarded as orthodox) apart from a case of papal heresy or crime. Yet this position was a commonplace of the apostolic movement and could find warrant in St. Bernard's *De consideratione*.[9]

Later that same year, it would appear, Gerson produced his first extant academic work *Pro unione ecclesiae* (*Oeuvres*, d. 253a, 6:1), which opens with a forthright declaration that "doctors" (theologians) share with the bishops in the rule of the Church. He is supporting the efforts of Nicholas of Clemanges and his own master, Pierre D'Ailly, to justify the entrance of his university of Paris into the prohibited open discussions about reuniting the Church.[10] First he notes that after the body of prelates, the university, as the Church's foremost theological body, enjoys the greatest "authority" in matters of faith. His basic principle is that after prelates, the Church's doctors have the greatest obligation to procure the Church's union, because after prelates, they have been "commissioned" with "rule" in the Church (*eis commissum est regimen*; *Oeuvres*, d. 253a, 6:7). The boldness of the position consists less in the flat claim, often if more cautiously advanced earlier in the theological tradition, than in the legal language deliberately chosen. He continues: "whence they have authority from the Church to determine scholastically what is true and what false." While "scholastic" should differentiate their determination from the "authoritative" decision to be rendered by the prelates, who alone can publicly command the faithful, can it be purely accidental that the word "authority" eases back into the role of the theologians? He seems clearly to imply that the hierarchical function is really secondary and executive. Here one sees, for apparently the first time in his thinking, a clear resonance of the traditional apostolic demand for the precedence of faith and the doctrine which teaches it over hierarchical authority in the healing of the Church's schism.

One is startled to hear from the fledgling theologian another, even bolder apostolic note: that in the name of this common good of believing all must be ruled, even the Roman pontiff, whom a simple layman has then the right to reprove (*Oeuvres*, d. 253a,

6:13–14). He has particularly in mind the not-so-simple layman, the French king.[11] Quite strong here already is the apostolic sense that the *community* of the Church arises in faith and in response to faith, and that faith grounds a primordial equality.

At this point Gerson is a conciliarist only in the sense that, like so many others of his time and earlier, he sees a council as the only appropriate means to heal the schism (*Oeuvres*, d. 253a, 6:10). But he does not advocate the calling of such a council, since there seems no way for a united council to gather. In company with Clemanges and D'Ailly, he is hoping to forestall precipitate moves on the part of the royal court towards a forced settlement in favor of Avignon (the so-called *via facti*).[12] After urging the king in his sermon to act, Gerson now wants him to stop the Orleanist campaign against the Roman claimant and to listen to the university's theologians. Upon Clement's death in 1394, Benedict XIII is elected and in the changed circumstances the university is once again allowed to discuss the schism freely. By this time Gerson has become chancellor of the university and must take a position. It was not a propitious time for an idealist to hold that office. The university, like the French nation, had become self-absorbed as one consequence of the great war with England, and, having lost so many recruits with the additional trauma of the schism, had become almost wholly a French institution, swept along by the interests of the French clergy. The tide which was to become known as Gallicanism was swiftly moving in.[13] Now his reformer's sense, having first spoken in support of the university's voice in the problem of the schism, finds itself drawing back from the university's course when the latter joins the French clergy in the campaign of the Duke of Burgundy's faction to bring royal pressure upon Benedict to resign.[14] His notes, made while the university was preparing a referendum as to what course should be pursued, the *De subtractione schismatis* (*Oeuvres*, d. 254, 6:22), show him totally out of sympathy with these maneuvers. Questionable and unrealistic tactics are not his idea for ending the schism.

With an assembly of the French clergy in February, 1395, mention begins of a possible subtraction of the obedience of the French church to Avignon.[15] In his sincere concern for the unity of the Church, which he sees receding even further, Gerson is totally opposed to this proposal, but he is helpless against the drift of opinion. On September 15, 1396, an assembly of prelates, abbots, and university delegates representing the French church was falsely reported to have voted subtraction in a tally manipulated by the Burgundian party.[16] But the outcome was inevitable. Claiming the invasion of immemorial liberties, a subsequent council of clergy voted in 1398 for total subtraction of obedience to Benedict XIII, the first manifesto of Gallicanism.[17] At this point Gerson seems to have retired from the fray, residing mostly at his living in Bruges.[18] His only recorded thoughts at the time about the schism are pastoral reflections on how best to preserve the Church's faith and life in this time of trouble (*Oeuvres*, d. 256, 6:29).

Chapter 3

Development

There is no question that Gerson's thinking underwent significant development during his years of comparative retirement in Paris. Earlier, reacting perhaps to the university's headlong plunge into subtraction, Gerson had found that his own thinking had come more and more into agreement with Benedict's position, whom he had defended against the demand for resignation (*De papatu contendentibus*; *Oeuvres*, d. 254, 6:24). In that work he had doubted that any valid election could follow even a double abdication, since the college of cardinals would not give its undivided consent. His thinking at this point still moves along ordinary institutional possibilities. He is not yet thinking of the possible prerogatives of the Church as a whole, moving outside ordinary institutional procedures. When after this period (in 1402) he returns to the fray, there is a new tone, signalling a development in his thinking.

The movement is not noticeably in a conciliar direction, but rather in an intensity and range of apostolic concern. There is, for instance, his concern for the communitarian nature of the Christian life. In a sermon preached on Holy Thursday, 1401, he alludes to the ceremony of the washing of the feet, observed on that day: "For those washed clean (*ablutis*) through grace all things are in common" (*Oeuvres*, d. 236, 5:411).

And he does not at all restrict these *communia* to the internal and purely spiritual. Citing Acts 4:32, which refers to the common possession of all goods, he says: "What else for those who come together than that their inheritance should be wholly one, their headship [i.e., with Christ] a common headship" (*Oeuvres*, d. 236, 5:411). He surely means Paul to be taken literally (2 Cor. 7:4): "The same man [i.e., Christian] is at once rich and poor, as the Apostle says, having nothing and possessing all things" (*Oeuvres*, d. 236, 5:416). And yet even here is a hint of conciliar things to come: all share the headship of Christ.

In the meantime, changes had also taken place in the political situation. Events had moved from an initial disaster for Benedict to a position of advantage. For purposes of self-aggrandisement at the expense of Burgundy, Duke Louis of Orleans took up Benedict's cause and the *via facti*—the plan to use force against the Roman claimant. In defence of their policy, the Burgundians sent royal officials, who appeared in Avignon on September 1, 1398, and forced Benedict to withdraw into the papal palace under seige. He would remain there several years, physically a prisoner to French royal policy.[1] But the Duke of Orleans, appointed guardian of the captive pope in 1401, never ceased to work for the restoration of obedience to him.[2] Meanwhile the subtractionist ecclesiastical arrangements had not gone well,[3] and the stridency of Cramaud's university policy was driving its theologians into the papal camp.[4] "Supporters of Benedict, and men like the theologians Pierre D'Ailly and Jean Gerson who refused Simon's canonistic theory in principle, had only to bide their time until changes in Paris or Avignon would allow them to demand an end to the totalist program."[5]

In April, 1402, Jean Courtecuisse, as spokesman for the Cramaud party, called for a general council of the Avignonese obedience to judge Benedict on charges of heresy and perjury.[6] Gerson's sense of responsibility as chancellor would not allow him to remain silent, and he ended his retirement with two publications, both in 1402, the *Replicationes* (*Oeuvres*, d. 258, 6:39) and the *De schismate* (*Oeuvres*, d. 259, 6:42). The interest of these two pieces for our theme lies in the indications they contain that his thinking in the interim had become more transcendental, so to speak. He is even more removed from the contingencies of the moment, more mistrustful of short-sighted practical moves, more averse to factionalism, more historically minded. His reflections all center on his concern for the unity of the Church, which he sees arising only from the whole, its restorative power not available to partisan maneuvers. When it is argued in behalf of a council of the Avignonese obedience that the cardinals of Benedict can be won to the idea, Gerson retorts that history shows that cardinals are not the only successors to the apostles. Before there were any cardinals the whole clergy, indeed, the whole body of the faithful, elected the pope. How could the cardinals have a power that did not belong to the whole Church (*Replicationes; Oeuvres*, d. 258, 6:39)? This vein of argumentation traces characteristically not to the institutional theological tradition but to that of apostolic protest, a reformist vein clearly more apparent in Gerson since his retirement to Bruges. It did not at this time coincide with any notable development in his conciliarism. In the *De schismate* he not only denies that a general council is expedient at this time but points out, rather unexpectedly, that in matters of fact and positive law—everything, indeed, apart from pure matters of faith—a general council, and thus the Church, can deceive and be deceived, however innocently (*Oeuvres*, d. 259, 6:47).

Since mention has here been made of "expediency," it should at once be pointed out how superficial it is to accuse him and other conciliarists (as once was the fashion) of throwing together a jerry-built ecclesiology to meet the desperate circumstances of the Church.[7] An inspection of almost any of his writings will show how far from basing his position on mere expediency is Gerson, for whom nothing is expedient which does not arise from the needs of the Church's unity and charity (e.g., *Oeuvres*, d. 253a, 6:8–9). It *is* true that the apostolic strain in him has early disposed him to relativize Church structures. In his earliest extant theological writing, the *Pro unione ecclesiae*, he has this very interesting conclusion:

> Whence in a case of necessity for procuring the common good of the faith almost all ways which otherwise would be illicit become licit because of the necessity of the good which is procured. (*Oeuvres*, d. 253a, 6:12)[8]

When he finally launches out into a thoroughgoing conciliarism, he does so because he regards it as a demand arising from the Church's *already existing* unity and the prerogative of that unity, as will be hereafter shown.

It must by this time have been clear to those around him that Gerson was convinced both of the legitimacy of the Avignonese

Benedict XIII and of the illegitimacy of all moves made against him, whether to force him to abdicate or to call a council to depose him. But his defence of Benedict should not obscure the new note that has appeared in his Church thinking, the "transcendental" note which appeals to ultimate realities beyond the Church's institutional procedures, the new more "apostolic" tone.

In a third treatise written at this time in defence of Benedict, Gerson sounds for the first time another apostolic note: poverty. In *De concilio unius obedientiae* (*Oeuvres*, d. 260, 6:54) he turns again to history for his justification of poverty, in the traditional manner of apostolic protest. In this "history" of papal temporal possessions from the time of Christ until his own time he means to show the contingency of their association with the life of the Church. It is his opinion that reform and withdrawal from temporalities to the level availing before Gregory the Great, or before Constantine's gifts to Sylvester, or even to that obtaining at the time of the apostles (!) might be necessary. There is here a passage that deserves extensive quotation:

> For it is clear . . . that the pope is able to remain universal pope in great perfection, indeed greater than Sylvester had; and nevertheless he would have no actual exercise of the temporalities of the universal Church throughout the dioceses, however much he would have dominion or the fullness of power by prerogative [*in habitu*]. This power can for specific causes be restricted and restrained, and indeed it should be, lest it be actually employed so that individual offices would not be left free to administer their particular temporalities [*immo debet ne exeat in actum sed dimittat singula singulis ministrare*]. Was Christ not the most perfect pope? Was not Peter likewise? But they abdicated every use in such things, although Christ could have obtained it with the greatest ease. Therefore the status of the Supreme Pontiff is in no way diminished in its perfection if for reasonable cause such anxious solicitude for such immortal responsibilities most perilous to soul and body should be removed for a time or suspended in its exercise of distributing and conferring temporalities. The perfection of such a status would rather be increased and he should certainly be thankful in the Lord. (*Oeuvres*, d. 260, 6:55–56)

The headlong rush of ideas seems to indicate an inner vehemence, a need to vent long-pent convictions. It is an extraordinary outburst from such an established churchman. Of course he was being influenced by the situation created in the distribution of the temporalities of the French Church by the years of the withdrawal of obedience from Avignon, years in which Church and government officials were at loggerheads dividing the repossessed spoils of the Avignon benefices.[9] But two significant matters here emerge. The first is the application of the scholastic distinction between habit and act to the office of the papacy, the first theoretical dissociation Gerson practices upon the conception of the papacy in its relationship to the life of the Church. The pope's fullness of dominion over the Church's temporalities *must* for good cause be denied its exercise and be transferred to individuals to administer. The very phraseology, the mention of the long-controverted "fullness of power," suggests that Gerson might be already prepared to extend the principle beyond the question of temporalities.

The other matter is the summoning of the old and famous Franciscan poverty-controversy standard of the "poor use" of Christ and the Apostles.[10] While carefully avoiding the Spiritual Franciscans' claim that Christ and the Apostles owned nothing, Gerson declares that they relinquished the use of what was in the case of Jesus full dominion over material goods. Where the Franciscan controversialists claimed that Christ and the Apostles relinquished all ownership, Gerson is content to say that they surrendered the *exercise* of a *fullness* of ownership, a characteristically moderated version of the apostolic protest, but nonetheless a determined one. He is more concerned with the spiritual connection between Peter John Olivi's "poor use"[11] and prelacy than in supporting a claim which had been condemned by John XXII,[12] the value of which had by his day become an empty shibboleth among the generality of Franciscans. We shall see that Gerson seems disdainful of the current Franciscan influence in the Church.

While one sees emerging here an explicit desire to control the papacy, the dominant concern is reformist: the yearning for an apostolic spirit in the conduct of the Church's highest office. Clearly, in defending Benedict's claims Gerson is no enthusiastic papal partisan. But while the subtraction of French obedience endured, he had no high hopes for the ending of the schism.

Events developed to encourage him. Probably with Orleanist connivance, Benedict had escaped his beseiged palace at Avignon (March, 1403) just as the French bishops' disillusionment with the interference of the divided royal court in the Church's affairs had served to encourage the growing sentiment in favor of ending the subtraction. The latter was accomplished on May 28, 1403.[13] On June 4, Gerson "celebrated the triumph of his cause"[14] by preaching his famous Pentecost sermon, *Emitte Spiritum Tuum*, one of his most moving treatments of a theme which was to become increasingly important in his ecclesiology: the Church as the body of Christ enjoying the outpouring of the Holy Spirit (*Oeuvres*, d. 225, 5:255–65). The spiritual-mystical conception of the Church will serve him, as it had so many other "apostolic" men, in the theoretical moves involved in relativizing and overleaping the Church's institutional procedures.

A later sermon, this time preached in the presence of Benedict during a Paris delegation's mission to the papal court at Marseilles (*Oeuvres*, d. 214, 5:110), is, perhaps understandably, filled with fulsome praise of Benedict, possibly in the hope of inducing him to magnanimous behavior. At any rate it appears to have met with his approval since he subsequently bestowed upon Gerson two Paris benefices.[15] Benedict's approval is surprising: under the sugar-coating Gerson inserted some startling language in great prophetic denunciatory style:

> [The Church complains:] Lo how almost all the ornaments of my earlier institution, discipline, and beauty have been turned into their opposite, while for the crown of humility the filthy dust of vanity, for the flowers of spirituality only the dung of temporality are embraced. There is erected over me a wisdom which is animal and earthly and diabolical, while that which is from above, peaceful and modest, is repudiated. (*Oeuvres*, d. 214, 5:117)

A work of his written at about this time gives even clearer signs of the growing need of his thinking to relativize office in the Church, specifically the papal office (*De restitutione*; *Oeuvres*, d. 262, 6:64). The requirement of utility in the Church, he there tells us, is the purpose of the papal dignity and may demand a restriction in the scope of papal activity, *especially* in matters not expressed in divine law (*Oeuvres*, d. 262, 6:64). He does not think such restriction derogates from the papal authority or the fullness of power conferred by Christ, who would not bestow power for the Church's harm, "for he might do what is evil and inexpedient for the Church." There is no denying that this is more a rationalization than a theological argument since utility cannot in the end be judged theologically but only practically. That he would subject the Church's highest office to such a standard says volumes about the progress of the disjunction occuring in his thought between the Church's spiritual realities and those obtaining in Church office. He is well on his way towards specifically conciliarist conclusions. We find him several months later using, apparently for the first time, the already famous slogan of the conciliar movement: the papal power was given for the edification of the Church, not its destruction (*Trilogus*; *Oeuvres*, d. 264, 6:81).

During these months Gerson had been part of the papal entourage travelling around the Rhone valley, where he no doubt had had many opportunities of observing the pope at close range, very likely a disillusioning experience.[16] At Tarascon on the Feast of the Circumcision, January 1, 1404, the sermon he delivers before the pope (*Apparuit gratia Dei*; *Oeuvres*, d. 212, 5:64) has a startlingly sharper tone. With all of its specific proposals and detailed criticisms it is nothing less than Gerson's first sustained apostolic protest. He surveys an ecclesiastical system choked with human laws and devices such as the excessive use of censures, "dead human laws" instead of the "living law founded in the eternal law and in equity or *epikeia*" which teaches that law is perfected and fulfilled when it is ordained to a higher end, "which end is charity according to the Apostle; otherwise Christ would rather have dissolved the old law than fulfilled it" (*Oeuvres*, d. 212, 5:73). (The much-discussed matter of *epikeia* will be treated in a later context.) His is an appeal to the divine law and especially Scripture:

> But let experience be asked what peril, what evil and confusion contempt for Sacred Scripture brings, sufficient as it

certainly is for the governance of the Church, otherwise Christ would have been an imperfect legislator. (*Oeuvres*, d. 212, 5:74)

But there are those who do not hesitate to consider the Church better ruled by human inventions than by the "divine and evangelical law" (*Oeuvres*, d. 212, 5:74). It is the evangelical law which teaches that he who would be greater among you must be the least of all and their servant. This he says clearly pointing the matter in the pope's direction.

Perhaps the boldest thing he has to say in the pope's presence is also the most severe disjunction Gerson has up to this time declared between the human and the divine in Church office: that the salvation of the Church is ordered absolutely and essentially only to God and *de ordinata lege* (by the ordained divine law) to the man Christ, but only accidentally to a mortal pope (*Oeuvres*, d. 212. 5:85). Here again we see the emerging association of a conciliarist direction with the intensification of apostolic concern. After all this it is difficult to believe that Gerson was as surprised as he says he was that Benedict removed one of the benefices he had recently granted him.[17]

Exasperation with the Avignon pope, who began to prepare an expedition against Rome, grew again in the French church,[18] and again there was a movement for subtraction of obedience stirring in the university, which produced a French Council's decision for partial withdrawal of obedience (November, 1406).[19] Again Gerson is opposed on principle, but is just as much out of patience with Benedict, and concurrently with the French Council he produces his *Acta quaedam de schismate tollendo* (*Oeuvres*, d. 266, 6:102). Here is the decisive break with his previous attitudes towards the prospect of a council. He formally sets aside the positive law of the Church concerning councils in the name of unity and by the authority of theology which is "superior and architectonic" in regard to lesser laws. The canonists' dictum that the presidency of the Pope is essential for a general council must be abandoned. In notes made at about the same time he suggests that a general council could be called of either obedience, without the pope presiding. (The Roman claimant, Innocent VII, had just died.[20]) Previously opposed to all forced cession, he now thinks that it is not repugnant to the divine law that Benedict—however much he be true pope—could be required by circumstances to resign (*Oeuvres*, d. 266, 6:102). In any case he is quite prepared to ignore Benedict in the opportunity opened by the Roman vacancy. He counsels that the French king should instigate a meeting between the two obediences before any election takes place and without consulting Benedict. Indeed Benedict himself had asked the Roman cardinals not to proceed to an election. But before his envoys arrived at Rome, a new pope had been elected, Gregory XII (1406–15).[21]

As it turned out, Gregory was personally impressive and favorably disposed to compromise, so that the French court decided to open official negotiations with Rome for the first time. In March, 1407, an embassy including both Gerson and D'Ailly was dispatched with instructions to visit both Popes and urge upon them the way of cession. Both sides refused. Rebuffed in the Spring of 1407 by Benedict (who had meantime entered into an agreement with Gregory), the embassy also failed that summer with Gregory. It had to content itself with waiting for a scheduled meeting of the two rivals at Savona, which never took place and probably was never intended to take place.[22] David Knowles describes the maneuvers of the two rivals during these years as "a long series of sidling advances, not unlike that of hostile cats."[23] The hesitations and evasions did not arise purely out of mutual antagonism or solely from personal ambition. Along with everything else it is after all understandable that neither of the rivals was willing to submit himself to the judgment of the body of cardinals to which each regarded himself as superior.[24]

February of 1408 found Gerson back in Paris.[25] Apparently no external pressures could be expected to work, especially since recent impasses had begun to look like the result of collusion between Rome and Avignon.[26] The general despair had begun to reach inside the two curias, where alone, by internal revolution, hope for change could find anchor.

At last a fatal blunder was made, and it was made by the Roman claimant. Gregory's consistory of May 9, 1408, in which he created new cardinals, apparently convinced his cardinals that he intended to perpetuate the schism; and nine or ten of them fled secretly to Pisa (where the rivals had previously agreed to meet, until both had again temporized).[27] There they issued an appeal for a general council and they were soon joined by most of Benedict's cardinals, whereupon Benedict fled to his native Perpignan. The assembled cardinals wrote to the emperor Sigismund, the kings of France, England, Hungary, Poland, all sovereigns and bishops, announcing their intention of convoking a council.

With the assembling of the Council of Pisa in 1409 "Gerson finally made his own breach with the theory of papal supremacy over the Church,"[28] or at least became a public and convinced conciliarist. The preparations underway for the assembling of the council moved him to launch into his first spate of formally conciliarist writings, which reveal from the start a full-blown conciliar theory, gathering up much of the conciliar arguments of the past generation and providing many interesting ideas of his own. That theory is virtually complete and quite consistent from this time through the writings at Constance. Thus this presentation can move from the development of Gerson's thinking to a more synoptic account of its apostolic emphases.

Chapter 4

Apostolic Notes

It will be useful to keep in mind in the following discussion the tone and content of the first of Gerson's "Pisa writings," the *Rememoratio agendorum durante subtractione* (*Oeuvres*, d. 268, 6:108), written, according to Glorieux, probably in July, 1408 (Glorieux, 108), and thus on the eve of his explicitly conciliar writings. It can hardly be called a conciliarist document at all, but perhaps can be viewed as Gerson taking stock of his concerns for the Church before plunging into the conciliar fracas. It was evoked from Gerson by his concern for the people of the French church during the period now beginning when the court, trying to bring Benedict to heel, had incurred his interdiction of the whole kingdom. A temperate, detailed and generous program for reform down to the parish level, it signals that Gerson sees the current struggle not as one for legitimacy but for the reform of the Church, which must always care in the first place for the Church's unity and charity. It will be seen how often Gerson appeals to that unity and charity as ultimate justification for the theories he proposes and the action he espouses.

Evangelical Law and Theological Leadership

To assess the scope of Gerson's apostolic approach to the solution of the papal schism, one has only to unfold all that is implicit in his recurrent appeal to *evangelical law*. To find a solution to her problems the Church must return to the purity of evangelical law, to adhere before all else to the law of God given in the Scripture. The Apostolic Church is the Church of the Scripture. We have already seen that his first sharp words of rebuke to the Avignonese pope on the state of the Church were based on the desertion of evangelical law (see p. 26 above). It will be noticed that the mention or invocation of evangelical law occurs regularly in the statements cited below.

Gerson's concern for evangelical law is apparent in the way he defines ecclesiastical power:

> Ecclesiastical power is power which has been conferred by Christ supernaturally and specially upon the apostles and disciples and their legitimate successors ... according to the evangelical laws for the attainment of eternal blessedness. (*Oeuvres*, d. 282, 6:211)

These evangelical laws are to be, and first of all, the primary concern of theologians. The "power" possessed by doctors, that is, theologians, to which he had referred in his first theoretical treatise, is this power given according to the "evangelical laws." At Constance also he speaks of the "power" doctors have of "interpreting and determining Scripture" and now calls this function "doctrinal" (*doctrinaliter tractare materias fidei*; *Oeuvres*, d. 273, 6:150).

The exercise of authority in the Church must be strictly according to Scripture. Papal decretals and bishops' synods have spiritual efficacy in the Church's life only to the extent that they are expressions of evangelical precepts. Speaking the language of scholastic theology Gerson actually calls the evangelical laws the "formal cause" of ecclesiastical power (i.e., that which makes power *ecclesiastical*; *Oeuvres*, d. 273, 6:194).

Thus, before all else, evangelical law must be enshrined and observed. Specifically it must preside over and control human law in the Church. Since the presence and importance of canonists within the life of the Church arise only in function of the Church's temporalities (as Gerson understands the matter) he sees only problems when canonists attempt to preside over Church law in general.

His concern here is only an apostolically heightened presentation of the struggle of the university theologians against the ever-more predominant influence the canon lawyers were exerting in the institutional life of the Church. Both disciplines, theology and canon law, had come to a first maturity within the same generation (roughly towards the middle of the twelfth century) but the impact of the initial Gregorian reform as the century progressed had become institutional rather than religious,[1] concerned with the universal hegemony of papal power. Its effect was to push the developing canonical science into an institutional dominance which, to the chagrin of the theologians, it never subsequently lost during the Middle Ages. When Gerson complained at Constance of "this multiplication of constitutions" he was voicing a traditional theological complaint.

If the evangelical law should be the heart of Church legislation then manifestly it should belong to theology to decree concerning all Church law, since it is the architectonic science in interpreting lesser laws according to the order and end of charity and unity (*Oeuvres*, d. 97, 3:161). Without this theological ordering, "positive constitutions" go astray and get involved in "inextricable difficulties," as in the present schism (*Oeuvres*, d. 266, 6:102).

> Wherefore theology, which is the evangelical law—I should better say its teacher and explainer—should in all things precede ecclesiastical prelates in their constitutions and decrees, lest they impede the precepts of God on account of a burdensome multitude. (*Oeuvres*, d. 97, 3:163)

The Teaching and Preaching of the Faith

We have seen above that Gerson accords theologians office in the Church (see above, pp. 27–28). Other theologians had wished to counter the influence of lawyers without taking this position, clearly of an apostolic cast. Here is surely not the bias of the theological pedant. Those who have read Gerson's sermons and instructions to the theological students of his day do not need to be told that he constantly warns them against the vanity of intellectual curiosity in questions of faith and the futility of acrimonious hair-splitting.[2] Nor do those who have read his mystical theology need to be informed that the true depth of faith is reached not by intellection but by charity.[3] His concern for the proper dissemination of the Faith proceeds not from the academician's love of erudition but the apostolic's love of the Gospel.

The subordination of canon law here finds an additional *institutional* rationale: the canons, he says, are only conclusions elicited or inferred from theological principles, that is, from the gospel and the other books of Scripture (*Oeuvres*, d. 222, 5:223). That would seem to be the reason why he thinks that a theologian can more easily comprehend canon law than a canonist in regard to theology (*Oeuvres*, d. 222, 5:227). And for this reason theological understanding must remain in control of canonical applications, as "in defining what is meant by heresy, heretic, simony, simoniac, etc." (*Oeuvres*, d. 222, 5:228).

As the years pass this concern for the centrality of evangelical law in the Church leads Gerson to point out more insistently the possible conflicts between divine and human in the Church when "human traditions" are not seen as relative to the variety of time and place. The pope and others should not impose "positive canons and other human traditions" rigidly everywhere. This, he says, drove the Greeks to depart from the Latins and causes daily much litigation and serious scruples. "You make null the command of God because of your traditions" (*Oeuvres*, d. 102, 3:299; cf. Matt. 15:6).

Doctrinal functions, being necessary to the preached word, can be attached to the apostolic mission. Echoing the words of 2 Timothy 4:2, Gerson says that the University of Paris knows herself to have been placed "by order of the Apostle" to be able "to exhort in sound doctrine" (*Oeuvres*, d. 210, 5:46). And this association introduces one of his most interesting ideas about the doctoral function: even if only by an indirect contribution the theological doctor is a successor to Paul in the office of preaching (*Oeuvres*, d. 288, 6:284).

Preaching is here at the center of his concern, a duty assigned centrally to the hierarchy, though the doctor "prepares" the preaching. Preaching is the most important of the prelate's work (*Oeuvres*, d. 282, 6:215). The Church is to be reformed as it was originally formed, on faith. "But the holy seed of this generation [i.e., of the Church] is the word of God, or faith." It is his settled conviction that preaching, not administration, is the primary duty of prelates. His *De desiderio episcopatus* (*Oeuvres*, d. 104, 3:329) is a striking illustration of his concern for episcopal preaching. The desire to be a bishop must be motivated before all else by the love of God and neighbor; in fulfillment of this love the first intention must be "to be able to preach more efficaciously or to admonish toward virtue." Commenting on the Scriptural text about the prudent and faithful servant, Gerson lists as the first mark of episcopal "prudence" that "he know the divine Scripture." When he looks at the bad among bishops he sees first of all those who are ignorant of divine Scripture and don't want to know it,

> who despise sacred Scripture even in its professors; who think it sufficient if sacred Scripture is studied and preached through others when nevertheless the obligation of knowing it has been annexed to such an office; who deny Sacred Scripture is necessary among those already of the faith. (*Oeuvres*, d. 104, 3:333)

Those are all but two of his specific criticisms, a quite unusual emphasis on the bishop's duty to preach. Students of conciliarist history have not always taken this concern for the supremacy of Scripture seriously in conciliarist writings.[4] Absorbed in the legal theory under discussion they tend to regard the scriptural language as mere window-dressing.

Again, his concern is different from that of the radicals of the apostolic movement only in that he entrusts this fundamental work almost exclusively to Church office, seeing the charisms (again) as endowments meant to adorn the mission of office, not to replace office in the life of the Church. The Church hierarchy has for him the pseudo-Dionysian triple mission of purgation, illumination, and perfection in regard to the lower orders. It is interesting that while the first and third functions are accomplished mostly in the conferring of the sacraments, the function of illumination is accomplished "through preaching and doctrine" (*Oeuvres*, d. 282, 6:219). The function of purgation is preparatory and dispository. For the work of perfection that of illumination is foundational and constructive. The foundation is the Word of God and faith.

In the light of these priorities, Gerson was to find Constance a disheartening experience. It seemed to him that the Church's prelates thought and acted more like lawyers (and politicians) than like theologians. He will speak from Constance with a note of weariness and disappointment at the endless legalistic squabbles he was witnessing. What point is there, he asks, in this multiplication of constitutions to be imposed on the necks of the faithful, when the Gospel is neither known nor observed? It is only animal and earthly wisdom to ignore "the law of the king" [the Gospel of Christ] to shore up papal decretals and the synodal constitutions of diocesan bishops. "The wine of Sacred Scripture and theology" were temporal goods enough for the Church (*Oeuvres*, d. 281, 6:193–94).

Perhaps in reaction to these evidences of evangelical neglect, at Constance he seems to shift his expectations for the doctrinal welfare of the Church away from the bishops and more towards the theologians. Where earlier he had described the determining function of theologians as "scholastic" (see above, pp. 26–27), he now comes to see their function more in terms of preaching: they prepare the doctrine which is to be preached. As mentioned above, at Constance also he speaks of the "power" doctors have of "interpreting and determining Scripture" and now calls this function "doctrinal" (*doctrinaliter tractare materias fidei*; *Oeuvres*, d. 273, 6:150).

But in the end this apostolic concern for preaching tends to detach itself from any particular office. It is highly significant that Gerson mentions lay preachers or "narrators" to whom, sometimes more than to many clerics, an explicit knowledge of the faith pertains (*Oeuvres*, d. 280, 5:187). One could hardly ask for clearer evidence of the influence of the apostolic movement than this acceptance, however restricted, of one of the most controversial and yet persistent practices of that movement, that of lay preaching.[5] It would be pressing the available evidence much too far to suggest that Gerson envisioned such preaching as anything to be regularized in the Church, but it is clear that he is concerned not so much with who does it, as that it be somehow done. And as he had insisted that doctors truly preach by their teaching, he is willing at last to agree that perhaps lay persons and even bishops (!) can fulfill the doctoral function, the latter at least by applying penalties to error (*Oeuvres*, d. 273, 5:152). Indeed when he sees that the council is in danger of being persuaded by the canonists that all decisions about the faith should be restricted to the Holy See, he fights for the magisterial rights of the bishops.[6]

Since with human beings matters are never entirely as they should be, Gerson knows that besides preaching and the evangelical law human beings need human discipline. He offers his own theory as to the origin of legal canons within the Church. The multiplication of canons originated with the multiplication of men within the Church who were gainsaying the evangelical law. Thus the Lord had need of canonists even in spiritual rule because theologians strictly so-called never sufficed (*Oeuvres*, d. 222, 5:224). The regrettable necessity of there being defective and contrary human beings in the Church means that there must regrettably be human (canon) law! Here speaks not the sophisticated legal thinker but the theologian in the mold of Augustine. And withal he is quick to warn us that

> The Lord does not want canonical regulations to have the same fixity as the evangelical law. Canon law must give way to *epikeia* and equity on penalty of invalidating God's law, according to Matt. 15:6. (*Oeuvres*, d. 222, 5:228)

(The matter of *epikeia* will be taken up presently.) In the end he wonders if canonical regulations have done more harm than good:

> What are so many traditions but so many snares, chains and nets to catch and bind the feet of the humble willing to walk according to the law of perfect liberty [of Christ]? Is not the Church, which was meant to be totally spiritual, totally heavenly, thus fallen by wretched happenstance into total brutal sensuality? (*Oeuvres*, d. 238, 5:439)[7]

Gerson sees the distinction between divine and human in the Church as central to a solution and remedy for the Church's ills. Posthumus Meyjes notes that "the idea according to which the Church is a purely spiritual power because it owes its origin to God, and as such bears a perfect character, consequently not needing any addition of a temporal nature, seems fundamental to him."[8]

The understandable concentration of so much of the conciliar research of past decades on the legal and constitutional theory implicit in conciliarist positions here can be seen to stray from a more balanced view. As has been said more than once here, Gerson was indeed quite at home in legal and political theory, which, like so much else in his polemical armory, he was quite willing to insert into his manifestoes for reform. But it should be clear that his conception of spiritual power will not allow one ultimately to *explain* his conciliarism in terms of a "doctrine of rights," amid the alternatives of a "corporatist" and an "individualist" political ideology.

Poverty and Power

With this consideration the question must arise: how does Gerson regard the whole question of temporal power as it confronts the apostolic appeal to poverty within the Church? Is he here also in the tradition of apostolic protest? Again the answer must take note of his institutional understanding of apostolic reform: not how that reform will replace the institution but how the institution will embody the reform. Gerson shared the conviction of the apostolics that Christ and after him Peter neither possessed nor desired temporal power. Posthumus Meyes is certainly correct in noting that Gerson sees the root of canonical thinking in the fact of the Church's temporal power and associates the emergence of the "completely new clan of canonists" with an excessive historical increase in that power (Posthumus Meyjes, 91–92). With the apostolics, he takes a historically conditioned view of the place of temporal possessions and power in the Church. With Constantine and following his donation, the Church began more and more to resemble a state in power and possessions (*Oeuvres*, d. 260, 6:54).[9] Unlike the radicals Gerson does not decry this development, instead considering it providential. The Church needed these new tools to aid in its missionary expansion (Post-humus Meyjes, 92). Nevertheless he sees that a time came when the increase in temporal power had become excessive and there occurred a certain "cooling" of holiness (*Oeuvres*, d. 260, 6:55). This latter term recalls a like phrase of Gerson's "dear" Bonaventure: "and thus, when charity had cooled down (*caritate refrigescente*) the Holy Spirit arranged that the Church should abound in temporal goods."[10] Franciscan influence on Gerson in the person of Ockham has already been noted, but this Bonaventuran influence in the Franciscan understanding of the evangelical significance of poverty clearly draws Gerson into the apostolics' orbit of concern about the negative effects of her temporalities upon the Church's true life. The

Church ought to give testimony of the need to be poor in the things of this world. He sees begging as a truly apostolic service to the Word. At Constance he will say:

> The need to beg [mendicitas], it has truly been preached, is the only or at least the principal means for fecundating the Church through the seed of the word of God, because riches, he says, suffocate the seed of the word. (*Oeuvres*, d. 234, 5:385)

What he disapproves of, he there adds, is only that begging which proceeds from avarice. This fact should be borne in mind when one reads some of his scathing comments upon the presumptions of the mendicant friars.[11] (It should also be noted that, for Gerson and many others, resentment against the friars is a form of protest against papal encroachments upon the rights of ordinaries.)

But here it seems one should say that his concern for this specific reform is rather marginal. He does not seem to have much confidence in the evangelical *power* of this kind of witness, perhaps because it had been so often compromised and made an object of ridicule by the behavior of many in the orders of friars supposedly committed to it. In any case he has a surprisingly indulgent attitude to the Church's temporal posture in this matter of property and power, perhaps to be mildly characterized as a general spirit of realism in his acceptance of the Church's great temporal power and influence. He thinks the Church may rightly wield temporal jurisdiction and hold worldly possessions, may even exert coercive authority in the world, *if secular princes have bestowed such upon her* (*Oeuvres*, d. 222, 5:212). By *such* endowment the Church can even imprison, levy fines, and confiscate goods. Gerson does not seem embarrassed to make such admissions. He is concerned about one thing especially: to make clear that such power is extrinsic to the Church. Indeed the Church would be more credible in imposing these penalties for purely temporal violations than by resorting to her own spiritual sanction of excommunication, thereby debasing it (*Oeuvres*, d. 222, 5:218). One wonders whether this indulgence might not have mostly a political motivation: not to affright virtually the whole hierarchy of the Church, particularly the French hierarchy with its Gallican tendencies, by demands for sweeping renunciation. Whatever may be the explanation, nothing could more clearly demonstrate that, while he is in the tradition of apostolic protest, Gerson is far from being a radical. He is concerned to recall the Church to its evangelical function, not to condemn in the name of the Gospel the structures of temporal society when they involve the Church.

Natural Law

The appeal of the conciliarists to natural law has often scandalized critics. It was, however, nothing new, as will be explained. And it is especially erroneous to see its introduction as an evidence of the secularization of the Church, as political and social interests attempting to enforce a solution of the papal schism. The conciliarists considered the appeal to natural law to be a bulwark precisely against the dominance of human law *within* the Church. Gerson's appeal is clearly motivated by protest against the encroachment of Church law upon the evangelical good of the Church. Of course this is a strategem to relativize and even set aside any particular positive law in the Church which he deems harmful to its unity and charity (see, e.g., *Oeuvres*, d. 273, 6:150). This had long been a strategy used in apostolic protest. The association of natural law with divine law and the Scriptures was by this time a long-established tradition, used originally by sectarian Christianity to minimize the positive law of the institutional Church. Reinhold Seeberg notes that the sectarians in general united natural law with the Gospel law in a revolutionary sense.[12] Ernst Troeltsch (*Social Teachings*, 1:349) sees this emphasis upon natural law as a judgment against the positive law of the Church. If in no other way this association of natural law and divine law would have come to Gerson from his familiarity with Ockham's thought, here as elsewhere influential in his thinking. In *Dialogus*, pars I, lib. 6 (p. 630), Ockham speaks of the divine law as comprised of "Scripture or right reason." Right reason it is which recognizes the natural law. In *Dialogus*, pars III, tr. II (pp. 932–33), he makes the association explicit, including all the modes of the natural law in the divine law. His purpose, like that of the sectarians, was to relativize and override the positive laws of the Church. This essentially philosophical move seems of course a piece of rationalism, thus of secularism, but the ancient sectarians would hardly have agreed with that characterization. And the sectarian origin of this association should not be regarded as tainting its nature as genuine apostolic protest, however one regards the justice of sectarian claims. They themselves regarded their protest as genuinely evangelical. It was probably inevitable that a reformist temper, sensitive to the disparity between divine and human in the Church, would summon to the aid of Scripture, where not sufficiently explicit, divinely-given "right reason" and the natural law which it acknowledges.

Only a more modern mentality would see natural law as secular. For the medieval mind law was something to be *declared* (not devised) by authority, and all authority came from God. Certainly Christian thinkers esteemed what was agreed to be the law of creation above all human declarations of law. Natural law was no more "secular" to this way of thinking than was creation itself. It was not a curious juxtaposition that Ockahm contrived when he coupled divine and natural law.[13]

Epikeia

The most celebrated use of natural law among the conciliarists, notorious, perhaps, because of its very generality and adaptability to so many practical purposes and outcomes, is the originally Aristotelian notion of *epikeia* (equity). Aristotle invoked it to remedy the corruptions and adjust for the imperfections of human positive law, the inevitable imperfections of which have always exercised legal thinkers. Positive law ought always to strive to approach the perfection of natural and divine law as far as possible, and natural law comes to its aid in the notion of *epikeia*. *Epikeia*, or equity, measures the distance between the "spirit" of the law (judged generally by the *intention* of the law-giver) and the actual situation of its literal application in a particular case. The imperfection of human law is precisely that it cannot accommodate every practical situation with complete fairness and adequacy. This disparity between legality and fairness is remedied by executive authority, which can adjust the law to the situation by consulting its "spirit" and overruling its letter (to whatever extent necessary). This was not to be regarded as a derogation from justice but a remedy, drawing positive law to the higher end of divine law. Gerson regards the proper use of *epikeia* in regard to Church law as itself a use of divine law; and this is so because epikeia draws law to the higher end of charity (*Oeuvres*, d. 212, 5:73). Seen as a "divine" remedy for the corruption of the Church, *epikeia* was a natural tool of apostolic protest; and to the extent that the conciliarists saw it that way, they must all be regarded as "apostolics."

Conciliarist writers[14] had earlier found Scriptural warrant and direction for the use of *epikeia* in Paul, who admonished that all authority is for edification (2 Cor. 10:8). The divinely revealed purpose of all law in the Church, the purpose to which *epikeia* must be applied, is the building up, not the destruction of the Church.[15] Positive Church law is of itself only human and must be judged in the light of the divine purpose, with *epikeia* the means for correction and adjustment. *Epikeia*, Gerson says, rules canon and civil law in regard to the Church through the divine and natural law. Thus *epikeia* is a rule used by theology, not a substitute for theology (*Oeuvres*, d. 272, 6:142). The theologians (for this is their role) *doctrinally* manage this *epikeia* to cut through all the obstacles of positive law; and only subsequently is judgment open to the experts in canon law (*Oeuvres*, d. 272, 6:138). The use of *epikeia* should be founded in "eternal and immutable rules of divine law" (*Oeuvres*, d. 272, 6:143–44). It should not be used casually and without reason; otherwise the stability of the law will be compromised (*Oeuvres*, d. 272, 6:145). It is thus a mistake in this context to accuse Gerson (whatever may be said of others) of expediency and opportunism. In his advocacy and defence of the use of *epikeia* he insists that such use be truly *theological*, not stemming from purely human prudence:

> If the prudent man should base himself only on experience in contempt of what the divine law says can and cannot be done, he easily deceives himself, as I know has happened among some . . . founding themselves in false principles. (*Oeuvres*, d. 272, 5:153)

Epikeia is founded in law, not lawless expediency.

As early as 1402, in the years before he became a conciliarist, Gerson the reformer explained the papal prerogative in the light of the end and purpose of law (bringing the matter thus within the domain of *epikeia*) and pronounced the right, using *epikeia*, to derogate from positive law in regard to the papacy:

> The papal dignity . . . has been established by Christ for the utility of the Church; wherefore this dignity ought to moderate its scope of activities [*agibilia sua*] according to the requirements of the utility of the Church as to its end, especially in those things which have not been expressed in the divine law. . . . Nor in this is there derogation from the papal authority nor the fullness of his power conferred by Christ, but it is fulfilled. For who would believe that . . . to be able to do what is harmful and inexpedient for the Church is a prerogative conferred by Christ? (*Oeuvres*, d. 262, 6:64)

Gerson here is speaking of a dignity "established by Christ," and thus a matter of divine law. And he allows the human posessor of this dignity to practice on his own initiative a restrictive moderation. To be noted is the nuance involved in the expression "*especially* in those things." Gerson clearly implies that sometimes even divine prerogatives must be adjusted to the utility of the Church. Apostolic protest could never equate the divine prerogatives of individual authority with those of the Church as a whole. At the foundation is always the community-reality of the Church. That reality, Gerson implies, might come before even some matters of the divine law. Indeed sometimes epikeia may be *equivalent* to divine law: "Canon law must give way to *epikeia* and equity on penalty of invalidating *God's law*, according to Matt. 15:6" (*Oeuvres*, d. 222, 5:228, emphasis added).

More startling, though less noticed, is the attack Gerson directs against some of the more extensive claims made for the sanctity of Church law. Gerson accuses the canonists and ecclesiastics of sometimes abusing Church authority by arrogating to it what belongs only to divine law, claiming a right to impose obligations seriously binding the conscience.

Evangelical Liberty

In this context arises one of Gerson's most noteworthy discussions, which, as much as any other, establishes his identification with classic features of the apostolic protest. It occurs in the midst of an extensive examination of the various laws present in the Church and the nature of the obligations of conscience which arise from each. This discussion constitutes his longest academic work, the *De vita spirituali animae*, six "Readings" produced in the period January–July, 1402, and thus before his "conciliar" period (*Oeuvres*, d. 97, 3). Here Gerson shows the traditional character of his churchmanship. He makes no attempt, in the manner of so many of the apostolics, to construe Church authority as simply the authority of Scripture. The Church is a polity as well as a mystical body, having many laws (a point he also makes in *Oeuvres*, d. 282, 6:225). After establishing those types of law which only can be truly called divine, he distinguishes the sorts of power which the pope possesses in comparison with those obtaining in human polities.

In the fourth Reading, it becomes apparent that these laborious distinctions are so many arrows in his anti-canonical quiver. There he makes it clear that Church law as such does not and cannot bind the consciences of believers under the penalty of serious sin. The reason: the Christian gives his conscience only to the law of the Gospel. Serious sin attaches only to the breaking of divine law, occurring only when there is some admixture of or connection with the pure law of God (*Oeuvres*, d. 97, 3:161). Thus in one of his corollaries he says:

> The omission [by the clergy] of the canonical hours, a transgression of ecclesiastical fasts and in general the transgression of all statutes and rules and canons is never a mortal sin except insofar as it is found incompatible (*dissonans*) with preceptive divine law. (*Oeuvres*, d. 97, 3:160–61)

He is deeply concerned that the Church with its canon law has burdened consciences. The pernicious result of ignoring or despising the leadership which theology ought to have in the Church is that communities and consciences are disturbed, confused, and burdened. On the basis of canonical interests, ecclesiastics, abusing their power, want to have whatever they ordain, devise, or command taken for divine law to be observed under penalty of eternal damnation (*Oeuvres*, d. 97, 3:161).

For Gerson, the Church has of itself no authority seriously to bind the conscience. This was hardly a traditional view then, as it is not even now.[16] It was Aquinas' opinion, for instance, that Church authority within its sphere as coming from God is seriously binding upon the conscience.[17] But that is not the kind of thinking that comes easily to an apostolic reformer, who tends always to see the distance between the human and the divine. Gerson sees that distance acutely and is never finished warning prelates and canonists against the sin of the pharisees, that of laying heavy burdens upon the necks of men, when the Gospel is a law of liberty. He characterizes their attitude clearly:

> [There are] those who argue thus: there is no power but of God and whatever we command, we command in the place of God; whatever we order on earth that God approves in heaven; therefore all our precepts are divine and of an authority equal to the gospel. (*Oeuvres*, d. 97, 3:201)

This attitude was hateful to him because he saw in the ecclesiastical bureaucracy, especially the Avignonese curia, a suffocating hindrance to his practical pastoral concerns for the care of souls and the spiritual life, as Posthumus Meyjes notes (*Jean Gerson et l'assemblée de Vincennes*, 106).

The "Evangelical Law" of Liberty

In the face of ecclesiastical arrogance, Gerson proclaims the law of liberty, a reality of the Gospel which he might have learned from Ockham[18] but which, had institutional circles been able to foresee Luther, would have sounded within the institution like a peal of thunder.[19] This plea for evangelical liberty, so dramatic in the arsenal of Luther, is arguably the most "apostolic" thing Gerson said or could say.

His deepest indignation may perhaps have come from his conviction, justified or not, that the canonists would not even acknowledge that "the way of divine law should even be called juridical" (*Oeuvres*, d. 212, 5:439). By this he seems to have meant that they regarded the divine law as having nothing to do with the practical obligations of daily Christian life in the community of the Church. Their attempt to occupy the whole ground of Christian living produced in the minds of the faithful a "frightful disorder" (Posthumus Meyjes, 89). The light yoke of Christ and the law of liberty have become yokes of sin (*Oeuvres*, d. 97, 3:129). This theme of evangelical liberty, so explosive for the future, is part of a conviction which is distinctive to Gerson: that only the truths of faith create divine law in the Church.

It is Posthumus Meyjes' view that Gerson realized that he was the first strictly to tie the extent of purely divine law in the Church to the compass of the truths of faith (as in *Oeuvres*, d. 104, 3:336; Posthumus Meyjes, 98). Indeed he defines the notion of divine law according to the notion of faith (*Oeuvres*, d. 97, 3:136). His is a presentation of the priority of faith perhaps unique among orthodox scholastics, which helps to stamp his ecclesiology as apostolic. When Luther singled out the preaching and believing of the true Faith as the foundational mark of the Church[20] he was taking up a long medieval tradition, but it was in the main a tradition of protest. Gerson makes his own version of that protest. The correspondence between divine law and the truths of faith is a corollary of the idea that the Scriptures (containing the truths of faith) are the only divine law in the Church.

Gerson's triangulation of evangelical law—faith—liberty was bound to eventuate in a severe relativization of papal decrees and the canon law regarding the papal office. By now it should be clear that these relativizations are indeed consequences of a theology, not merely polemical positions in search of a rational justification. They are, moreover, a corollary of his apostolic understanding that Christ and the Apostles remain the standard and norm for the Church's life. That corollary states that the Church of later generations, the popes in later succession to Peter, have not the *same status as the foundations*. Along with the words of Scripture, the teachings and laws of the apostles handed down in the Church's tradition are divine revelation, and thus divine law (*Oeuvres*, d. 97, 3:138). The popes, councils, even the whole Church cannot make divine laws or change the evangelical law, cannot give new truths of revelation (*Oeuvres*, d. 97, 3:137–39; *Oeuvres*, d. 282, 6:224). The only absolutes in the Church are those matters which are necessary to the attainment of divine beatitude, and these only—revealed by God—are divine (*Oeuvres*, d. 97, 3:135). All else, and thus the authority of the pope and his decretals, are not absolute, although Gerson's cautious wording of this claim betrays his awareness that it may seem overbold (*Oeuvres*, d. 97, 3:134–35). Thus, in terms of the Church's divine mandate, every papal pronouncement has only a lesser claim.

The Church and the Papal Fullness of Power

Gerson, no more than Ockham or the generality of the conciliarists, was prepared to deny the canonized teaching of the papal fullness (*plenitudo*) of power in the Church. Christ, he says, established the Church as one supreme monarchy over all; and this, in the present divine order of things, cannot be changed or taken away (*Oeuvres*, d. 102, 3:298). He calls Marsilius of Padua a heretic for denying this authority to the papacy (*Oeuvres*, d. 102, 3:299). For Gerson, the internal hierarchical order of offices and administrations is not ordinarily at the Church's own disposal since it was given by Christ (*Oeuvres*, d. 271, 6:132). But like all the conciliarists and such an ancestor as John of Paris Gerson's presentation of the papal plenitude is scarcely calculated to fall pleasantly on curialist ears, or even those of canonical traditionalists. Like most of his conciliarist colleagues, he surrounds this monarchical plenitude with conditions and limitations which undeniably attenuate the doctrine. Perhaps his most generalized treatment of the relation of the papal plenitude to that of the Church occurs in one of his last conciliar writings (February 6, 1417; *Oeuvres*, d. 282, 6:211), where he says:

> The fullness of ecclesiastical power is formally and subjectively in the Roman Pontiff only. The fullness of ecclesiastical power is in the Church as in its end and as regulating the application and use of this ecclesiastical plenitude through itself or through a general council adequately and legitimately representing it. (*Oeuvres*, d. 282, 6:232)

Shorn of the technical language, his claim is that while the pope concretely exercises the Church's plenitude, he does so for an end which *only the Church as a whole* (or representatively in council) *may decide* and acting *under* the Church's regulation. It would be hard to defend this understanding of the papal plenitude from the canonical tradition, which arguably treats the papal plenitude as an independent *alternative* exercise of the

Church's plenitude. Clearly the pope's plenitude has not the full latitude as that of the whole Church, except that "in some way" he is its source (*Oeuvres*, d. 282, 6:232)! One could hardly make the case that his stirring apostolic and conciliar proclamations have escaped all muddle!

Another passage in an earlier work gives us his clearest, most specific, and, at the same time, most succinct statement of the relationship of the two plenitudes (*Oeuvres*, d. 271, 6:133). It pretends to a scholastic precision. He says that the keys were given to Peter to be exercised with authority (*auctoritative et exercitative*) but were given to the Church for universal custody (*universaliter et susceptive*), or they were given to the Church as her own proper faculty (*in actu primo*) and to Peter to be exercised by him in specific acts (*in actu secundo*). Here the subordination in his description of the papal plenitude does not appear, apart from his saying that the papal power is included in that of the council, although the pope has it in one way, the council in another, just as the keys were given differently to the Church and to Peter. Thus, he says, in many things which concern the pope, the council has an authority which is both advisory and peremptory (*dictativam*), while the pope's authority is one of execution (*exercitativam et executivam*). But then the analogy he draws makes the papal subordination quite clear: the relationship is like that in man between the deliberating and deciding mind and the acting and executing will (*Oeuvres*, d. 271, 6:133; *Oeuvres*, d. 214, 5:479).

The inevitable "apostolic" conclusion from this limitation of the papal plenitude is drawn by Gerson: whatever of divine authority is abidingly available to the Church rests ultimately only with the Church as a whole; only secondarily and with reservations does it lie with the supreme pontiff. Gerson moves from the divinity of the beginnings to the divinity of the whole. There is a curious passage in his exultant address to the English, where he has the imminent assembly of the council at Pisa in view. He says that the congregation of the Church is more greatly and variously endowed (*multiplicior*) over against its secondary (i.e., papal) head than is a civil congregation, since besides a natural unity and polity it has a supernatural unity and divine laws. These give it additional rights over its head (*Oeuvres*, d. 217, 6:131–32).[21] He neither explains this idea nor adduces any application, but he thereby draws a clear connection between the Church's supernatural unity and its capacity to act above, indeed without, its secondary head. (The Pisa assembly did not include either of the papal claimants nor did it enjoy their approval.)

The papal fullness of power and that of the Church are thus not convertible. Gerson's practical corollaries are much more precise than is his theory. He notes four important differences. (1) The Church's faith will not fail; this is not true of the pope. (2) The Church can regularly use the pope's power where the need arises; the converse in regard to the Church's fullness of power is never true. (3) The Church originally contains every kind of ecclesiastical power, even the papal, but not so the pope, who cannot absorb, e.g., the power of the bishops. (4) The Church can regulate and limit the pope's use of his power, but the pope may never judge the Church or limit its use of power (i.e., in a general council, *Oeuvres*, d. 282, 6:217). His final summation of the relationship between the two plenitudes is given in a memorandum of February 16, 1417: "Nevertheless we must say that [the plenitude] is everywhere more principally in the Church" (*Oeuvres*, d. 283, 6:251). Thus the pope's will is never the final court of appeal, "as though there survived no supreme test" (*Oeuvres*, d. 282, 6:218). While the Church or the general council cannot take away the papal plenitude it can put it under the restraint of "certain rules and laws (*Oeuvres*, d. 282, 6:218)."[22] This limitation is the "stable foundation" of all ecclesiastical reformation (*Oeuvres*, d. 210, 5:45). The essential point is that the final judge of such papal performance is the council, as the "inerrant Church" (*Oeuvres*, d. 102, 3:302).

From this prerogative derives the Church's right to correct or reprove a reigning pope, although Gerson characteristically prefers to base his argument on Scripture rather than deduce a position as a corollary from theory. His favorite text—a commonplace of the conciliarists—is Matthew 18:15: "If your brother sins against you, go and correct him." For Gerson this text founds in the Church the fullness of coercive power in the use of the spiritual sword over any Christian at all, who is our brother even if he is pope (*Oeuvres*, d. 282, 6:216). Just as the pope, however legitimate, is a son of the Church, so he can and ought to be called the brother of each and every man. Christ gave us to understand this when he taught us to pray: "Our Father," etc. If we all have one father in heaven and one mother on earth, the Church, we are surely all brothers of each other. To say this is not true of the pope is "the most patent nonsense" (*Oeuvres*, d. 286, 6:267–68). We have here an exquisite example of the mixture of values and motives in the conciliarists. In clear witness to the tradition of apostolic protest Gerson appeals to Scripture and to the conception of the Church as a community of brothers (!), all equal before God. At the same time the polemical value of such a levelling text would be too choice to neglect in bringing the *papa*, the "father," to heel.

We have seen that even in his first published treatise on schism Gerson maintained the right of the Church to correct the pope (see above, pp. 27–28). At the end of his conciliar career this idea has been distilled into axioms. "The Church is the judge of the pope whenever he sins publicly and has been denounced to the Church" (*Oeuvres*, d. 286, 6:274). But his approach is not as summary and radical as some of the axioms might suggest. During the last efforts to secure the deposition of Benedict XIII (January, 1417) he wrote that since the papacy is one of Christ's gifts to the Church, we ought to receive the "vicar of the spouse" with reverence, honor, and all benevolence, as long as he treats the Church even tolerably. We should call him father, honoring him as lord and head. But (and here Gerson uses the word for passing on a tradition, *trado*) we have been told that if the vicar grows cold and becomes an evil-doer (*maleficiatus*) so that he is incompetent (*inhabilis*) to the needs of the spiritual children of the Church, such a one should not be thought a worthy spouse of the Church or vicar of the spouse (*Oeuvres*, d. 281, 6:196).

Deposition of a Pope

Here one gets to the position many have thought radical and intemperate: that the pope serves conditionally, at the good pleasure of the Church.[23] It is true that occasionally, as here, when events tend to exasperate him, he strays from his usual moderation. As a rule Gerson contemplates the deposition of a pope only in serious circumstances. The common canonical tradition had always maintained that a pertinaciously heretical pope *ipso facto* ceased to be pope. Gerson rejects this position with singular vehemence, insisting that even such remains a true pope and an official act on the part of the Church is the only means to accomplish his destitution (*Oeuvres*, d. 102, 3:308). The "character" imprinted in baptism establishes the papal candidate, like any other Christian, in the unity of the Church, and that character is all that is required for him to become and remain pope, whatever becomes of his faith, until such time as he resigns or is deposed by definitive sentence. The reason he gives for his vehement rejection of the earlier opinion is the heretical Wycliffite association of dominion with grace which he sees in it (*Oeuvres*, d. 102, 3:309).

The Council, it must be remembered, was much exercised to condemn the Hussite version of Wycliffe's teachings, but here Gerson's dismissal of a famous tenet of the canonical tradition is indeed a bold declaration of theological independence. It is also true that he was out of patience with those who invoke the divine excommunication as an excuse for not proceeding against a pope and ending the scandalous division of the Church. To him, apparently, the theory (and excuse) of an automatic papal self-excommunication would deprive the Church of the ultimate exercise of its own inalienable fullness of power. Clearly he feels that those citing this canonical maxim are impeding the work of the council as they had previously blocked all productive attempts at unity (*Oeuvres*, d. 102, 3:312). For him there is no possibility that the Church can preserve her own good unless she is always mistress of her offices (*Oeuvres*, d. 102, 3:302) and this must entail that only the Church can, and the Church must, destitute an unworthy pope.

The consequence of this position, of course, is that a duly elected and reigning pope would not cease to be pope even after becoming a raving lunatic or raging criminal. Gerson has something like this in mind when he mentions the possibility of a pope being bound or imprisoned or thrown into the sea (*Oeuvres*, d. 102, 3:300, 309). De Vooght (41) refers to this passage among others in complaining of the "incredible violence" of some of Gerson's language. Gerson was here supposing a case where a legitimate pope attempted criminal violence against some person, who might justly repel the attack. If the supposition seems extreme it is hardly more so than the behavior of many a pope like Urban VI, which would have been known to Gerson.[24] It seems that "incredible violence" could be asserted of Urban VI.

With many other conciliarists, Gerson followed the canonical tradition of the later Decretists in affirming a variety of circumstances, first suggested by the great Huguccio of Pisa (with strict reservations not observed by later canonists), warranting the deposition of a legitimate pope, among them "prostitution, tyranny, mangling or flogging someone, dissipating goods, abusing" (*Oeuvres*, d. 102, 3:300).[25] He certainly believed that the recent history of the papacy afforded examples of all of these misbehaviors. At the Council of Constance on July 21, 1415, he said that the general council may depose a pope for any crime by which his behavior has notoriously and incorrigibly scandalized or is scandalizing the Church (something the council had just done in the case of John XXIII for his "notorious simony"). There he had solid canonical precedent. Tierney sums it up:

> The Decretists themselves did not explicitly formulate the doctrine of a judicial supremacy of the Council over the Pope [with the exception, he notes in a footnote, p. 67, of Alanus], but their assertions that the Pope could be judged *a tota ecclesia* and their views concerning the superiority of a Council in matters of faith could quite easily lend themselves to the conciliar interpretation—that the whole Church was possessed of an authority superior to the Pope's.[26]

It should be noted here that it was in this famous sermon on the Departure of Sigismund that Gerson emphasizes that the famous *Haec sancta* (more specifically and accurately referred to as *Sacrosancta*) decree proclaiming the supremacy of the general council was not borrowed from a canonical Gloss, but from the eternal Gospel.[27] He reaffirms three years later that this is the evangelical law, since Christ has told us that if a member of our body scandalizes us we should cut it off; and the pope is a member of the body of the Church (*Oeuvres*, d. 288, 6:284). But, if one does not take into account the actual situation of crisis, it would seem something less than cautious or moderate for him to say, as he did in the 1409 address to the English delegation, that the council can reject a pope duly elected and constitute another if that course "seems expeditious" to the edification of the Church (*Oeuvres*, d. 271, 6:133).[28] Reduced to the lapidary terms of an axiom the position certainly seems more radical: "The vicarious spouse of the Church can be removed even without personal fault, though not without cause" (*Oeuvres*, d. 102, 3:310).[29] Being useful to the edification of the Church would of itself hardly seem to rank a cause as sufficiently serious.

But such extreme statements are better understood against the background of the events of the schism. The great scandal was that relatively trivial but tangled contingent events had made it originally impossible for one to know which was the true pope, or indeed if either pope was to be followed. What made this papal schism intractable in so unique and unprecedented a way was that the two popes had been elected, as Knowles phrases it, not by different "parties or potentates" but by "the same very small body of men."[30] Divine providence itself, it appeared, had allowed trivial factors to confuse the most serious of all earthly pursuits, that of eternal salvation under the direction of God's vicar. This was not a situation to encourage the institutionally complacent but rather to call out reformist apostolic instincts. If God could allow such things to happen to His Church then there must be some appalling distance between its life and His will, so that that life must be seriously questioned.

And the confusion had not abated. In the years immediately following the onset of the schism, dozens of authorities on both sides were heard on the facts and the laws involved. Neither side had been able to emerge with a clear, exclusive claim to be in the right, though the preponderance of testimony seems to have slightly favored the Avignonese claim.[31] The succeeding decades brought with them additional events affecting the credibility of each claimant, heaping further confusion upon the original uncertainties. Mean little human contingencies had been providentially allowed to break for so long and for so many millions of souls the spiritual guidance of Christendom. If God could allow this, how could men in the Church not contemplate *any* strategies which might be able to restore order and unity? No informed observer by the end of the century could any longer hope that the tangle of claims about fact and law could be satisfactorily unravelled. No one could know which was true pope; and thus perhaps even the true pope would be obliged to resign, however genuine his claim and blameless his life.

Critics of a much later age might wonder at theories which called institutional pieties so severely into question, but they tend to forget that it was precisely the institution which had failed, leaving reformers the duty of calling every Church institution and office into question, in the name of the ultimate reality of the Church, which must lie beyond the corrupting reach of any institution or office. When one reflects upon all of this, it is not hard to understand how Gerson could maintain that the Church has a right to depose a pope "without fault, though not without cause." Such causes he mentions (*Oeuvres*, d. 102, 3:311) are: the hopeless detention of a pope by the Saracens; the loss of reason by the pope (alleged in the case of Urban VI); and the inability of the cardinals to vouch for his election before their deaths (which had been the case after Urban's election).[32] It seems obvious in these and other conceivable situations that the Church *must* have the power for good reason to depose even a legitimate and blameless pontiff. How much more, then, one who had richly earned his deposition?

All this reasoning is really nothing more than instructed common sense. It has the advantage, for those who are concerned to respect theological legitimacy as well as historical accuracy, of posing no clear obstacle—in the opinion of this writer—to a fair-minded reading of the actual development of the previous tradition in regard to the papal office. At least some conciliar propositions also would seem to present no problems for theology, for ecclesiology, or for the Scriptures. In the absence of a credible case for any such problem, and in the face of this impressive witness of the widespread apostolic movement, one is at a loss to explain the unyielding resistance of Church orthodoxy to this arguably inevitable move towards some sort of papal limitation. Did the medieval papacy generate for itself some kind of insuperable institutional fascination, some sort of *blik* which keeps modern commentators from a clear-sighted assessment? The treatment of conciliarism as enunciated in the Council of Constance still suffers from confessional concerns.

Chapter 5

The Church as Apostolic Council

One of the principal justifications which the first conciliarists had given for the possibility of a general council even if neither papal claimant would call one was a distinction made famous by the constant reiteration of Ockham in his vastly influential (and notorious) *Dialogus*[1] between regular and casual (i.e., exceptional or occasional) authority in the Church. While the pope regularly has the power to call a universal council, that power can be used by the Church as a whole for its self-preservation without a pope's authorization. But Gerson goes much further than this. When necessary, the universal Church can declare and determine "truths of faith either necessary *or useful* for the rule of the universal Church" even without his consent, and that infallibly (*De auctoritate concilii*; *Oeuvres*, d. 272, 6:115; emphasis added).

This is, indeed, an enlargement of the foundational principle of conciliarism: the full authority of the Church, apart, when necessary, from the pope, and, even without his consent, in this view even capable of infallible pronouncement when "useful." Bold and arresting as this position is, its interest in our context is rather its apostolic import, which appears clearly in what follows in the same text. There Gerson presents the interesting— and very un-Occamist—view that the Church gathered together has the authority of the universal Church not only because it represents the latter but because *it has this special privilege* (i.e., of bearing full authority) *from Christ*. He is not thinking here about office or structure in the Church: reaching back behind canon law, behind office and structure, he is summoning the traditional apostolic vision of the primordial apostolic Christian community, which already contained the powers of the church structures elaborated later. The Church in its inner being is always an

Chapter 5: The Church as Apostolic Council

apostolic council, able to act in its community wholeness to further its life and to preserve itself. *The gift of the council is already contained in the gift of community in the Church.*

The influence of Gerson in the opening months of the Council of Constance is sufficient testimony that the preponderating body of the council's various currents of opinion had already agreed to some fundamental tenets of the conciliar position. If later critics have considered Gerson's thinking extreme, the council in its earlier phases did not. As he points out, in the deposition of John XXIII the Council of Constance had vindicated its claim to be superior to the pope. He was not declared to be a self-deposed heretic. The council had proceeded against him with no claim either that he had become a heretic or that he had not been legitimate pope. The council had acted to *make* him illegitimate (*Oeuvres*, d. 288, 6:286). The reasoning was not simply that offered by Gerson at his council sermon delivered at the departure of Sigismund (July 21, 1415): If the sovereign pontiff can give a bill of divorce to the Church, spouse of Christ, as did Celestine, why cannot the Church give the same to the vicar of the Bridegroom, especially if there is cause?[2]

It may well be that the development of events had made such a deposition seem not at all a radical act. But if the council could act as the superior of a legitimate pope, it had to have reached the conviction that, representing the Church as a whole, it already possessed the papal power without him, and, so to speak, before him. Actually that conviction had already procured the assembly at Pisa in 1409, in which neither of the papal claimants would cooperate. The Church may in the absence of a certainly legitimate pope act in his place. Gerson makes this claim explicit in a way unparalleled in its forceful and far-reaching justification: the Church can do this because "the papal power has indeed been given to the Church itself and belongs to it as to the pope himself, although in different ways" (*Oeuvres*, d. 102, 3:304).

His explanation of this position is even more far-reaching. We have already examined a scholastic explanation he gave for the distinction between the papal fullness of power and that of the Church as a whole. In a sermon delivered at the council on January 17, 1417, Gerson offers another version in language even more intimidatingly scholastic. The supreme pontiff's fullness of power is *"subjective, ordinative, regulative, et suppletive"* (i.e., residing in him personally, for the purpose of giving order, regulating and supplying what is needed) over individuals in the Church, "but the Church gathered in council has fullness of power even over the pope *ordinative, regulative, et suppletive*" (Sermon *Nuptiae factae sunt*; *Oeuvres*, d. 234, 5:384)

Gerson sees that Thomas and Bonaventure (among others) seem to grant supreme and full (*plenam*) power to the Pontiff *restrictively* (i.e., to his office uniquely) but maintains that they were speaking only in comparison with "individual faithful and particular Churches" (*Oeuvres*, d. 234, 5:385). One can scarcely describe this as the usual understanding of the papal plenitude. In this understanding, for example, the Church, even without the pope, has a *constitutional* right to assemble itself—and here is his unique and arresting claim—because the Church is instinct with "the divine seed diffused throughout its body" (*Oeuvres*, d. 272, 6:134). It can assemble itself especially to provide itself with a visible head. This it does not to achieve unity but *in virtue* of the abiding essential unity the Church enjoys with Christ its spouse (*Oeuvres*, d. 272, 6:137):

> But if someone should ask what authority an apparently headless council without a pope depends on and uses, the answer is the authority of Christ its head and indefectible spouse. (*Oeuvres*, d. 102, 3:301)

The essential unity of the Church is irrefragable, abiding always with Christ its spouse, so that when there is no vicar—dead either corporeally or by civil law or when no one will obey—the Church can procure an undoubted vicar by congregating in a council which represents it with an authority greater than that of the cardinal-electors (*Oeuvres*, d. 272, 6:137). What he affirms of the papal office he applies to all other Church structures. Not only does the council already include the powers of the local Roman church, of the patriarchs, of the college of cardinals, but even of the episcopacy and the priesthood "in the same way," i.e., whether the members holding offices are present or not (*Oeuvres*, d. 282, 6:222).

Because of its unbreakable unity with Christ, the Church is always, especially in council, the apostolic community. For Gerson the council, by itself and without the pope, bears the full reality of that original community. However extreme this position might be deemed, it undeniably claims to fulfill the central demand of all apostolic protest: that the act of the Church be the act of the authentic apostolic community. In this sense it would be difficult to exaggerate the apostolic content of Gerson's conception of the authority of the council. It is a conception which unashamedly (and sometimes awkwardly) prescinds from the Church's constitution as though the latter, though divinely instituted, does not reach to the heart of the divine presence in the Church. It is a "trans-legal" conception which does not concern itself with possible legal conflicts. Before the Church is an institution it is the Mystical Body of Christ. As such, its assembly possesses divine life and fecundity within it.

This is where Gerson's Pseudo-Dionysian hierarchical doctrine seems to be inadequate to his concern. When he speaks of the ideal functioning of the Church he presents his Dionysian scheme. Thus in a memorandum for a projected sermon in 1409 in the presence of Alexander V (never subsequently delivered) Gerson believes he is addressing a situation of victory over the schism with the daunting prospect now looming of a thoroughgoing reform of the Church. Facing this he appeals to his Pseudo-Dionysian vision of the ideal Church and reminds the hierarchy that its work is to purify, illumine and perfect others in the Church in the cause of "heavenly order" (*Oeuvres*, d. 221, 5:212). There follow examples of all those who desert their proper places in the Church, creating that disorder which is at the root of schism. Indeed schism is but a further advance of an original disorder and conflict (Oeuvres, d. 221, 5:213–16). But in the context of the conciliar proceedings (originally the ill-fated Council of Pisa but actually at Constance), that orderly hierarchical vision seems inadequate to him.[3] He looks instead to the Church's primordial reality as the Body of Christ, Spouse of the Bridegroom, led by the Spirit. His early sermon to the Fathers of Constance (*Ambulate dum lucem habetis*; *Oeuvres*; d. 210, 5:43–44) speaks indeed of order in the Church, but not the Dionysian order; it is the Pauline account of First Corinthians of the gifts of the Spirit, all given to make the one body of Christ, whether gifts of office or the more spiritual gifts (1Cor 12). The Church of the Spirit is already instinct with all the gifts of the Spirit. How else could he say that the Council already includes the powers of the (absent) local Roman church, of the patriarchs, of the college of cardinals, even the episcopacy and the priesthood—whether the members holding offices are present or not (*Oeuvres*, d. 282, 6:222)?

Indeed, he states as a principle, that "the papal power has been given to the Church itself and belongs to it as to the pope himself, *although in different ways*" (emphasis added). This principle, along with the idea that the power of the Council is continuous, introduces a certain *doubling* into his conception of the Church function. Standing potentially behind the normal hierarchical function is something more primordial: the original apostolic council.[4]

A discussion of the "divine seed" mentioned above constitutes for us surely the most arresting thing Gerson had had to say to the English on their way to Pisa in 1409:

> We have besides a sort of formal cause, and one preparing in a life-giving way for the celebration of the council; which form is the living and efficacious seed of God, the seed of the Holy Spirit having the formative and reformative power of the whole unity, the whole body of the Church. (*Oeuvres*, d. 271, 6:126)

Gerson is very explicit that this seed is more ultimate in the constitution and unity of the Church than sacraments, or the hierarchy or its magisterium (*Oeuvres*, d. 131,6:297; *De Auferibilitate*; *Oeuvres*, d. 272a, 3:295). Clearly this quasi-formal cause of the Church is its originating reality in the founding act of Christ. It is ontologically prior to all office and structures which presuppose it and thus (in a Church founded upon the apostles) is the most *apostolic* reality of the Church. The Church is always the council of the apostles.

Subsequently he describes this seed as a spiritual power and a certain life-giving skill placed throughout the whole body of the Church, by which the hierarchical order is able to subsist till the end (*Oeuvres*, d. 102, 3:297). Mention of hierarchical order shows that in invoking this "divine seed" Gerson is not concerned to dissociate the action of the Church as a whole from any of its offices, not even that of the pope. His is, it bears repeating, an *institutional* version of apostolic protest, and his attaching the *generative* spiritual presence of the "divine seed" to the hierarchy is in striking contrast to the egalitarian instincts of the general body of apostolics.[5] He is rather concerned to emphasize that where matters which determine the Church's whole life of faith and charity are involved, the Church operates under the efficacious action of the Spirit, whatever the offices involved (*Oeuvres*, d. 253a, 6:9). The divine in the Church is never surrendered to human contingency.

Whatever else might be the function of the divine seed, Gerson emphasizes that it effects the unity through which it operates. It is active not only in the distribution of charisms and graces but as the Church's fullness of power (*Oeuvres*, d. 234, 6:385–86). The scattered Church has this power only in some material or potential sense, whereas the *congregatio* and *unitio* which comes about in a general council gives a quasi-form to this power (*Oeuvres*, d. 282, 6:217). The gathering of the Church into council is like the union of matter and form, the imperfect with the perfect (*Oeuvres*, d. 271, 6:127). The divine seed effects and preserves the actual inner unity of the Church. Ozment very perceptively calls this "semen" the "intrinsic charter of reform" for the Church in Gerson's thought and suggests a connection between his *synderesis* anthropology of the *via mystica* (its reformatory power for the whole soul) and the *semen* ecclesiology of the *via concilii*.[6]

This apostolic-communitarian vision of a transcendent unity in the Church gives us the best understanding of why the general council is for Gerson the supreme and clearest actuation of the Church's primordial nature and authority. The council is the whole in regard to which any particular structure of the Church is only a part. The pope is related to the Church as a part to the whole (*Oeuvres*, d. 282, 6:222). Indeed, as we have seen, the entire Church assembled representatively in council already includes the papal power whether the pope is present or not, and has the same authority over the Christian.

Perhaps nowhere has Gerson spoken his mind more impressively on the authentic nature of the Church than in his famous treatise *De auferibilitate sponsi*, written originally with the 1409 Council of Pisa in mind but directed finally to the Council of

Constance in the decisive weeks of March–April, 1415 (*Oeuvres*, d. 102, 3:294). A long quotation of 1 Corinthians 12:4ff. adduces the Pauline charisms, manifestations of the Spirit in wisdom, knowledge, faith, healing, prophecy, etc. as the privileged descriptions of the functioning of the Church, a functioning which describes her very constitution, giving it "integrity" and "perfection" (*Oeuvres*, d. 102, 3:296–97). It is true that he seems in this passage to regard these operations as belonging exclusively to the clergy ("the various members of the hierarchical grades of office," *Oeuvres*, d. 102, 3:298), but they are at the very least as evangelical a description of clerical function as a theologian of his day would think of taking from Scripture. But his definition of ecclesiastical power tends to draw it into association with the more general gifts to the Church as a whole (*Oeuvres*, d. 282, 6:211). He there describes this power as a "special gift" to distinguish it from the supernatural gifts given to every member of the Church, such as faith, hope, charity, prophecy, fear of the Lord, piety.

To be noted here is the lack of differentiation between the gifts of grace and the charisms, as if to say that what counts is the activity of the Spirit, not the particular modes of that activity. But especially to be noted is the bringing together of ecclesiastical power and the charisms as both "supernatural gifts," more a specific difference than the now-traditional contrast between office and charism. In the light of these assimilations it would seems that Delaruelle's judgment that laity and clergy constitute for him two absolutely heterogeneous milieux is a quite misleading over-simplification, while Oberman's statement that for Gerson the laity are simply auditors would surely have drawn from him vehement denials.[7] In a mature discussion of the procedures of a general council he insists that it is the prerogative of the council to give the vote to whomever it wishes.[8] It is unmistakeable that he intends to interpret (and judge) the Church of his day by the standard of Paul's descriptions of the Church at Corinth. To be sure, his institutional form of apostolic protest would abhor the attempt of the radical apostolics to dissolve office among the many charisms of the Church. But he clearly wants to focus attention on the charisms rather than the authority of ecclesiastical office. Indeed he wants to see the charisms as firmly entrenched in office itself, attached to the very function of office, to constitutionalize the charisms by "charismatizing" the offices. While all the laity possess charisms, the hierarchy must understand that it possesses them constitutionally for the official functioning of the Church. That is to say, the Church functions internally not by office but by the Spirit and spiritual charism. Reform will happen when the charismatic conduct of office is a reality. When Gerson's apostolic concern is focussed on practical measures to be taken in the ongoing life of the Church, understood as the functioning of the Spirit, his appeal is not *from* but *to* the hierarchy. Primitive perfection should rest with them since their offices "were primitively placed in the Church by Christ as in a kind of life-giving seedbed" (*in quodam seminario vivifico*, Oeuvres, d. 102, 3:297).

Perhaps the best way to highlight crucial features of Gerson's apostolic ecclesiology is to set the foregoing beside the presentation of that ecclesiology by Louis Pascoe.[9] In his effort to rescue Gerson from the lurid tones of "radical conciliarism," Pascoe follows the estimable work of G. H. M. Posthumus Meyjes in finding in Gerson a "firm exponent of a hierarchical ecclesiology" (Pascoe, 135). However, while he is careful to mark the reformatory concern in that ecclesiology there is a real problem in accepting his conviction that the hierarchical principle is "the primary principle of church reform" (Pascoe, 136). While his attention to a broader context than the supposed ties to Marsilius and Ockham (Pascoe, 135, n. 1) characteristic of earlier literature is praiseworthy, his exposition of Gerson's Pseudo-Dionysian schema is all too abstract and historically absent-minded about Gerson's developing commitment to the ecclesial crisis of his day. The fault lies, it would seem, in his thesis that Gerson's mysticism is the broader context for his ecclesiology and concept of church reform (Pascoe, 137).

Thus Pascoe takes us through Gerson's Dionysian-influenced cosmology of the heavenly and terrestrial worlds, from the Trinity to the "subcoelestial hierarchy" of the church on earth (Pascoe, 137). For Gerson there is a "close relationship between the celestial and terrestrial worlds in that the latter imitates and reflects the hierarchical order of the celestial realms" (Pascoe, 138; *Quomodo stabit regnum*, VII, n.980).[10] Now all this is instructive in its way but, it seems, ultimately beside the point. As the crisis of the Church moves to its climax Gerson's apostolic concerns are not from the hierarchical top down but the communitarian bottom up. He does not expect the hierarchy, for instance, to reform the laity anymore than he looks for the hierarchy to be reformed by the increasingly discredited Avignon papacy. It is true that he closely associates the "seed" of the Church with the ecclesiastical hierarchy, but is quite willing to see that seed operative anywhere in the ecclesial community, since the seed is ultimately the Holy Spirit.

The mistake comes in equating Gerson's practical religious concern for the Church with his immersion in mystical thought. It is one thing to lucubrate about the highest offices in the ecclesiastical hierarchy (papacy and cardinalate) purifying, illuminating and perfecting lower levels, and so on (*De potestate ecclesiastica*, VI, n.227), but Gerson sees too clearly that the present functioning of the Church is a travesty of this ideal picture, while not for a moment losing faith in it or its governance by the Holy Spirit. Unlike some other apostolics he knows not a "true" Church beyond the visible church, but a "divine" movement guiding and a divine "seed" able to "form and reform" the Church at any moment. While this "seed" is generally associated with the activity of the hierarchy, Gerson makes it clear that its ultimate source is the "universal body" of the Church (*De auferabilitate sponsi*, III, n.297). Indeed his many pleas and proposals to the Church through the years are unthinkable unless he clearly conceived of a potential functioning of the community of the terrestrial Church which lay beyond ordinary hierarchical procedures.

Pascoe misleadingly presents the emergency reformatory activities of the council as ordinary *hierarchical* moves (Pascoe, 142–43). Of course the Church in council will adopt traditional procedures (for the most part, but remember the strategem at Constance of the "nations" for diluting the power of the cardinals and curia). It remains true that the picture sketched by Gerson of the Church's inherent (if mostly potential) powers makes it clear that the hierarchical function is penultimate. Pascoe writes: "the union, love, and peace which represent the finality and reformative dynamism of the entire hierarchical order are clearly the results of the Spirit working through the hierarchical structure of the Church" (Pascoe, 142). Here he cites a passage from Gerson's address to the English on their way to the Council of Pisa. This passage makes no mention of the hierarchy, for the very good reason that Gerson is proposing a very un-hierarchical idea: that the Church has the power of the Spirit's semen to form and reform itself even if neither papal claimant or court is present at a Council. Thus he speaks not of the hierarchy but of "the whole body of the Church . . . through all of its joints" (Eph. 4, cited in VI, n.126).

Pascoe' regular insertions of the hierarchy into Gerson's discussions are indicative of the bias of his approach. They occur where Gerson—one may venture to say: deliberately—elides that mention. "Working through the hierarchical order," Pascoe adds in one passage (Pascoe, 143). But the passage of Gerson which he then cites does not mention the hierarchy but speaks instead of "this sacred synod . . . representing the Church which as spouse of the Bridegroom is *intimately* joined to him (*Sponsi Christi et Ecclesiae sponsae suae esset unus spiritus*; *Spiritus Domini*, G, 5, 521–22, emphasis added). This rhetoric seems intended in holistic fashion to *blur* hierarchical distinctions. Pseudo-Dionysius is no lover of the bridal mysticism! And here, Pascoe gives his peculiar and gratuitous exegesis: "the bishops and priests, moreover, as spouses of Christ and the Church."

Pascoe thinks that his study establishes "that mysticism alone provides the intelligible context in which [Gerson's] conciliarism and reform ideology can be fully understood" (Pascoe, 153). Whatever may be said about his mysticism as context for his "reform ideology," it seems, on the contrary, that, as it concerns conciliarism, Gerson's mysticism remained a surprisingly inert element and that the reform impulse actuating him during the papal crisis is something quite different from his Pseudo-Dionysian picture of the Church's *ideal* functioning. Steadfastly Gerson holds to that ideal picture (as Pascoe and others have established). But his reform appeal in the papal crisis is clearly not to the Dionysian ideal but to the "apostolic": to the primordial presence of the Spirit and the Bridegroom to be actualized most efficaciously in the enactment of a council. The tie is not between mysticism and council but council and apostolic protest.[11]

Thus the conciliarism of Gerson arises not out of his Pseudo-

Dionysian hierarchicalism nor from his mystical preoccupations. Those are the predilections of his contemplative theology and it is not amiss to discern many links and parallels between them and his ecclesiology (Ozment, Tierney, Posthumus Meyjes). They cannot, however, be said to drive his conciliar vision. This latter proceeds from a more visceral religious impulse, so to speak. The apostolic, communitarian spirit of reform in him, at last confronting the necessity of a general council, summons a more primordial, original vision of the Church's ultimate reality. Before the Church is a hierarchy, before it guides the mystical ascent of the individual soul, it is an apostolic council convoked by Christ and assembling in the Holy Spirit.[12]

This sharp turn in Gerson's ecclesiological utterances has scandalized many since his time (even the generous and sympathetic John Morrall). It has been partly responsible for the charges of radicalism, intemperance, Marsilianism, and so on. The need is not to deny the turn but to explain it. And the explanation is not the influence of Marsilius or Ockham, nor the rationalizing political opportunism charged by some of his critics (Ullmann). And it is obviously not the direct outcome, without remainder, of the previous canonical tradition. I would suggest that the explanation is found in the centuries-old tradition of medieval apostolic protest.

Such a conclusion does not, of course, remove all theoretical (indeed, logical) problems from conciliar thought. Morrall notes Gerson's "failure to draw the full logical consequence of his representative theories" and thus instances "a measure of ambiguity in the whole Conciliar position."[13] While I am not comfortable with that characterization of Gerson's positions as "representative theories," he is quite correct about the ambiguity. We have already pointed to Ockham's influential distinction between "regular" and "occasional" function in the Church, itself possibly the mother of all ambiguities adopted into the conciliarists' thinking. It is this same ambiguity, not susceptible of any theoretical regularization, which renders the ecclesiology of Ockham, himself *not* a conciliarist, ultimately incoherent.[14] One can speculate as to the root of this ambiguity in Ockham, whether his problems with Rome, or his philosophical prepossessions, etc., a favorite medievalist parlor game. As to Gerson it should be clear that he does not seem even interested in tracing the historical articulation of authority in the Church. Authority arises out of the founding will of Christ and the superintendence of the Spirit, which the Church can embody but never replace. As we have pointed out repeatedly, the implication of Gerson's thought is consistently that the regular authority structure of the Church does not reach to the Church's ultimate and primordial reality. It seems that Gerson is prepared to leave any anomalies, any theoretical awkwardness to be solved by the immediate guidance of the Spirit in the Church, the Church's seed.

This tradition of apostolic protest, while it may offer no practical blueprint for the on-going reform of the Church, can certainly provide the impulse, the values for such an effort, as in the first half of the fifteenth century it could have been more clear-sightedly followed for a more successful outcome to reforming efforts. That possibiity alone should justify the serious consideration of Gerson's conciliarism for its own sake as well as for a more accurate understanding of his work. Admittedly, it is not the task or the prerogative of this study to provide any practical outcomes. Historical studies can make no theological, ecclesiological claims. What they can do is serve historical probity, as well in the treatment of late-medieval conciliarism and specifically the case of Gerson as any other matter. That probity would appear to be in some short supply here. In this matter historical treatment is still plagued by confessional prepossessions.

Roman Catholic orthodoxy as presented in the thinking of more traditionalist theologians (Delaruelle, De Vooght, Joseph Gill, August Franzen) seems fixated, as observed in the last chapter, on the unquestionable validity of the strict, monarchical model for Catholic ecclesiology, with a papacy not quite absolute, but clearly more than constitutional. K. A. Fink's masterful account,[15] in deference to Roman Catholic orthodoxy but unwilling to compromise the morality of historical research, dances around the question of whether the decree on conciliarism had historical facts and ecclesiastical tradition solidly on its side. Where the materials attest clearly to a consensus in the contemporary view of the ultimate supremacy of the council he says so (Fink, 446–48) and decries the biased edition of the Constance decrees in the fourth edition of the *Editio Romana* of 1612. At the same time he allows for the claim of a "perhaps necessary and express approval" of the notorious *Sacrosancta* document by Martin V (never explicitly given). He artfully summarizes his interpretation by advising that the offending decree be gauged not by Vatican I but by its own contemporary milieu (Fink, 467). To this date the many editions of Denzinger's *Enchiridion Symbolorum*, which collects the official Roman decrees, make no mention of the solemn proclamation of conciliarism at Constance, instead reproducing only the condemnations of Wyclif and Hus, and the decree against the tyrannicide defense of Jean Petit.[16] Even the very respected David Knowles, cognizant of the preceding canonical tradition, much of which qualified the absoluteness of the papal monarchy, does not free himself from this fixation.[17] On the other hand Protestant-oriented writers (notably Walter Ullmann[18]) seem to regard the whole issue as theologically irrelevant to a Church which ought to acknowledge the Word of God as the only divine authority, a Word which is generally regarded as giving no fixed model for the constitution of the Church.

These prepossessions have as their consequences basic interpretive positions on the unfolding conciliar events. The Vatican, curialist position has always been: a truly radical schism *could not* have happened and therefore *did not* happen. There has always been one true pope (Urban VI of Rome) and only one legitimate line of papal succession (Urban's Roman successors). The Avignon claimant was and remained schismatic and the Council of Pisa was an aberration. Constance was legitimated only by the convocation pronounced by the Roman claimant, Gregory XII, before his subsequent free resignation. The official Roman position remains that only Constance decrees enacted "in a conciliar manner," can be accepted as legitimate. Among other requirements this entails that they must have been expressly ratified by Martin V, the undoubted, duly elected pope who ended the Council. The *Sacrosancta* pronouncement of conciliarism does not meet this requirement.

As to mainline Protestantism, and for that matter Protestantism in general, the story of conciliarism is only a penultimate demonstration of what could happen to a church which had long since followed a different lead than the Word of God. Ultimately, the whole question of "legitimacy" was a political matter as none of the claimants had ever truly been evangelically "legitimate" and conciliarism had been an answer to a question wrongly asked. One could of course attempt to assess the honesty, fairness, and even altruism of the various actors in the papal disputes. One might be tempted to consider that the Pisa and Constance conciliarists were more "right" than their opponents (as attempting to curb absolutism in the Church), but none of the reformers knew in the end what to do to heal or to reform the Church. Conciliarism and its outcome were really a political struggle whose aims can only be judged practically, or at best by one's own socio-political understanding.

Thus the basic prepossession of the Roman partisans is the indefectibility of the high monarchical view of the medieval papacy. The prepossession of those not of a Roman persuasion is the purely institutional, political nature of the struggle.[19] As to the outcome and its historical consequences, Roman partisans see the papacy emerge triumphant (after the collapse of the subsequent Council of Basel) from its most serious peril, armed now against all the onslaughts of a secularizing Western world.[20] The others (e.g., Walker and Lotz)[21] see the definitive defeat (after Basel) of efforts to make of the pope a limited, constitutional monarch, being won at the price of a fateful surrender of power over the Church to the monarchs and nations of Europe.[22]

These, of course, are not in principle exhaustive interpretations. It might, for example, be suggested that at least some conciliarist ideas could still have a future.[23] The present study might be accompanied by a suggestion that a reconsideration of them in the light of the long Christian history of apostolic protest could do much to reestablish their ecclesiastical legitimacy. Reluctantly but realistically, it has to be admitted that historical reconsiderations can here make only a limited contribution.

Notes

Notes to Introduction

1. Who does not recall the famous remark of J. N. Figgis that the *Sacrosancta* conciliar pronouncement is "probably the most revolutionary official document in the history of the world" (*Studies of Political Thought from Gerson to Ockham* [Cambridge: Cambridge University Press, 1931], 32)?

2. J. B. Russell, *Dissent and Reform in the Early Middle Ages* (Berkeley: University of California Press, 1965), 6–7, contends that they and kindred ideas alien to Christianity entered Western Europe only in the mid-twelfth century and that indigenous forms of unorthodox reformist dissent were an inevitable human by-product of "unselfish zeal for the reform of the Church."

3. See, for example, M.-D. Chenu, O.P., *Nature, Man, and Society in the Twelfth Century: Essays on New Theological Perspectives in the Latin West*, ed. and trans. Jerome Taylor and Lester K. Little (Chicago: University of Chicago Press, 1968), 203–69; Malcolm D. Lambert, *Medieval Heresy: Popular Movements from Bogomil to Hus* (New York: Holmes and Meier, 1977), 39, 43–44; Gordon Leff, *Heresy in the Later Middle Ages: The Relation of Heterodoxy to Dissent c. 1250–1450* (Manchester: Manchester University Press, 1967), 1:2, 29; Leff, "John Wyclif: The Path to Dissent," *Proceedings of the British Academy LII*, 153; Scott W. Hendrix, "In Quest of the *Vera Ecclesia*: The Crisis of Late Medieval Ecclesiology," *Viator: Medieval and Renaissance Studies* 7 (Berkeley: University of California Press, 1976): 348–66; Gordon Leff, "The Apostolic Ideal in Later Medieval Ecclesiology," *The Journal of Theological Studies*, n.s. 18 (1967): 58–82. Colin Morris, *The Papal Monarchy: The Western Church from 1050 to 1250*, The Oxford History of the Christian Church (Oxford: Clarendon Press, 1989), 341, points out that "the Gregorian programme provided an umbrella under which a variety of reforming groups could shelter." He and others describe several such groups which characterized themselves as "apostolic."

4. It would seem that the work of correcting this misunderstanding begins with the contribution of Albert Hauck, who appears to have been

the first to connect conciliar ideas with the mainstream tradition, specifically that of medieval canon law. In 1907 he proved the connection of these ideas with the twelfth century Decretists' commentary on Dist. 40, ch. 6 of Gratian's *Decretum* in his article "Die Rezeption und die Umbildung der allgemeinen Synode im Mittelalter," *Historische Vierteljahrschrift* 10 (1907): 465–82. The epochal work of Walter Ullmann on the canonistic sources of conciliar ideas laid the foundation for the definitive contribution of Brian Tierney in his classic *Foundations of the Conciliar Theory: The Contribution of the Medieval Canonists from Gratian to the Great Schism* (Cambridge: Cambridge University Press, 1955).

5. Heiko A. Oberman, *The Shape of Late Medieval Thought* (Edinburgh: T&T Clark, 1986), 30–31, citing Hermann Heimpel, ed., *De modis uniendi et reformandi ecclesiam in concilio universali* (Leipzig-Berlin, 1953), 13.

6. Tierney, *Foundations of the Conciliar Theory*, esp. 47–67.

7. Leff, *Heresy in the Later Middle Ages*, 1:2, 29; Leff, "John Wyclif," 153; Antony J. Black, *Council and Commune: The Conciliar Movement and the Fifteenth Century Heritage* (London: Burns & Oates, 1979); Leff, "What Was Conciliarism? Conciliar Theory in Historical Perspective," in Brian Tierney and Peter Lineham, eds., *Authority and Power: Studies on Medieval Law and Government* (Cambridge: Cambridge University Press, 1980); Hendrix, "In Quest of the *Vera Ecclesia*," 348–66; Leff, "The Apostolic Ideal," 58–82. Antony Black, in conversation with the author about this traditional religious background, remarked: "We still haven't got it [i.e., medieval conciliarism] quite right."

8. Black, *Council and Commune*; Leff, "What Was Conciliarism?"

9. John B. Morrall, *Gerson and the Great Schism* (Manchester: Manchester University Press, 1960); P. Glorieux, "La vie et les oeuvres de Gerson," *Archives d'histoire doctrinale et letteraire du moyen age (1450–51)*, 149–92; L. Salembier, "Gerson," in Charles G. Harbermann, ed., *The Catholic Encyclopedia*, 15 vols. (New York: R. Appleton Co., 1907–12), 6:530–31; J. L. Connolly, *John Gerson, Reformer and Mystic* (Louvain: Librairie universitaire, Uystprovst, 1928); James K. Cameron, "Conciliarism in Theory and Practice 1378–1418" (Ph.D. Diss., Hartford Seminary Foundation, 1953); Steven Ozment, "The University and the Church: Patterns of Reform in Jean Gerson," *Medievalia et Humanistica: Studies in Medieval and Renaissance Culture*, n.s. 1 (1970): 111–26; Louis B. Pascoe, S.J., *Jean Gerson: Principles of Church Reform* (Leiden: E. J. Brill, 1973); G. H. M. Posthumus Meyjes, *Jean Gerson: zijn Kerkpolitiek en Ecclesiologie* (The Hague, 1963).

10. Salembier, "Gerson," 530.

11. For these concerns of "apostolic" renewal, see Chenu, *Nature, Man, and Society*, 203–69; Rosalind B. Brooke, *The Coming of the Friars* (London: George Allen and Unwin Ltd., 1975), 22; Ernest W. McDonnell, *The Beguines and Beghards in Medieval Culture* (New York: Octagon

Books, 1969), 5–36, 141; Lambert, *Medieval Heresy*; Morris, *The Papal Monarchy*, 29–30, 341, 468, 497. Louis B. Pascoe, S.J., has a preliminary consideration of this idea in "Jean Gerson: The *'Ecclesia primitiva'* and Reform," *Traditio* 30 (1974): 379–409. See also note 3 above.

Notes to Chapter 1

1. Burton, *Dissent and Reform*, 5, regards this "Great Reform Movement" as emerging in the eighth century "with the mission of Saint Boniface and his associates."

2. Ernst Troeltsch, *The Social Teachings of the Christian Churches*, trans. Olive Wyon (London: George Allen & Unwin Ltd., 1931; Harper Torchbooks edition, New York: Harper and Row, 1960), 1:329.

3. Colin Morris, "Medieval Christendom," in Geoffrey Barraclough, ed., *The Christian World: A Social and Cultural History* (New York: Harry Abrams, Inc., 1981), 136. Morris notes that from 1045 onwards, the popes chose names recalling those early days: Clement, Damasus, etc.

4. Hendrix, "In Quest of the *Vera Ecclesia*," 352.

5. *Epistola apologetica pro ordine canonicorum regularium* (in Migne, *Patrologia latina* 188, 1125 C, 1136 C) written about 1150, cited in Giles Constable, "The Diversity of Religious Life and Acceptance of Social Pluralism in the Twelfth Century," in Derek Beales and Geoffrey Best, eds., *History, Society and the Churches: Essays in Honour of Owen Chadwick* (Cambridge: Cambridge University Press, 1985), 37.

6. In Migne, *Patrologia latina* 170:611–64. Cited in Hans Küng, *The Church*, trans. Ray and Rosaleen Ockenden (New York: Sheed and Ward, 1967), 345.

7. Troeltsch, *The Social teachings of the Christian Churches*, 1:330.

8. F. Tocco, "Gli Apostolici e Fra Dolcino," *Archivio storico Italiano* 19 (1897): 241–75; E. Anagnine, *Dolcino e il movimento ereticale all' inizio del trecento* (Florence, 1964). Both cited in Hans Wolter, "The Crisis of the Papacy and of the Church, 1274–1303," in Hans-Georg Beck, et al., *From the High Middle Ages to the Eve of the Reformation*, trans. by Anselm Biggs, Vol. 4 of Hubert Jedin and John Dolan, eds., *The History of the Church* (New York: Seabury Press, 1980), 243.

9. See note 7 to the Introduction above.

10. Francis Oakley, *The Medieval Experience: Foundations of Western Cultural Singularity* (New York: Charles Scribner's Sons, 1974), 70.

11. Lambert, *Medieval Heresy*, 39, 43–44.

12. Gerhart B. Ladner, *The Idea of Reform: Its Impact on Christian Thought and Action in the Age of the Fathers* (Cambridge, Mass.: Harvard University Press, 1959). For the tenth century in particular see André Vauchez, *La Spiritualité du Moyen Age occidental: VIIIe–XIIe siècles* (Paris: Presses universitaires de France, 1975), 33–74. Yves M. J. Congar, *Vraie*

et fausse réform dans l'Église, 2nd edition, *Unam Sanctum* 22 (Paris: Editions du Cerf, 1968), describes the apostolic characteristic of reform as it generally recurs throughout the Middle Ages.

13. Chenu, *Nature, Man, and Society*, 203–69. For developments continuing into the thirteenth century, see Congar, *Vraie et fausse réform dans l'Église*. See also L. M. Dewailly, O.P., "Notes sur l'histoire de l'adjectif 'apostolique'," *Mélanges de science religieuse* 5 (1948): 141–52; M. Mollat, "La notion de la pauvrete au moyen age," *Revue d'histoire de l'Église de France* 149 (1966): 1–17; Janet L. Nelson, "Society, Theodicy, and the Origins of Heresy," *Studies in Church History* 9 (1972): 65–77.

14. John McManners, ed., *The Oxford Illustrated History of Christianity* (Oxford: Oxford University Press, 1990), 211.

15. Oakley, *The Medieval Experience*, 70.

16. Migne, *Patrologia latina* 182:915, quoted in Russell, *Dissent and Reform*, 7–8. Ironically, Bernard was speaking of the most famous of early reforming monasteries, Cluny.

17. Chenu, *Nature, Man, and Society*, 219; Wolter, "The Crisis of the Papacy," 240–46.

18. Leff, *Heresy in the Later Middle Ages*, 1:2, 29.

19. Lambert, *Medieval Heresy*, 44. In Brittany at the turn of the eleventh and twelfth centuries a "multitude of hermits" was to be found in the woods, some of whom would travel widely, barefoot and preaching; see Brooke, *The Coming of the Friars*, 49.

20. Those men and women who had forsaken homes and possessions to follow Robert of Arbrissel, later the founder of the famous Fontevrault nunnery, called themselves 'Christ's Poor.'

21. It should be noted that early in the thirteenth century Innocent III several times gave official permission for laity to preach, whether within their own groups or on restricted subjects, e.g., penitence, Brooke, *The Coming of the Friars*, 81–87.

22. R. W. Southern, *Western Society and the Church in the Middle Ages*, Vol. 2 of *The Pelican History of the Church* (Hammondsworth, Middlesex, England: Penguin Books, 1970), 242.

23. Leff, "The Apostolic Ideal," 72.

24. Chenu, *Nature, Man, and Society*, 241–42; Leff, *Heresy in the Later Middle Ages*, 2, 7.

25. Margaret Aston, "Popular Religious Movements in the Middle Ages," in Barraclough, *The Christian World*, 169–70.

26. Morris, *The Papal Monarchy*, 468.

27. James of Vitry, *Historia occidentalis*, xxxiv (ed. John F. Hinnebusch), 165–6, cited in Constable, "The Diversity of Religious Life," 45.

28. Leff, "John Wyclif," 153.

29. See especially John Moorman, *A History of the Franciscan Order from Its Origins to the Year 1517* (Oxford: Clarendon Press, 1968).

30. The story is ably and carefully told in Malcolm D. Lambert,

Franciscan Poverty: The Doctrine of the Absolute Poverty of Christ and the Apostles in the Franciscan Order, 1210–1323 (London: S.P.C.K., 1961). See also L. D. Douie, *The Nature and the Effect of the Heresy of the Fraticelli*, Publications of the University of Manchester, Historical Series, 61 (Manchester: Manchester University Press, 1932).

31. Gerald Strauss, *Manifestations of Discontent in Germany on the Eve of the Reformation* (Bloomington, Ind.: Indiana University Press, 1971).

32. Glenn Olsen, "The Idea of the *Ecclesia Primitiva* in the Writings of the Twelfth Century Canonists," *Traditio* 25 (1969): 84.

33. Leff, "The Apostolic Ideal," 71.

34. Lester K. Little, *Religious Poverty and the Profit Economy in Medieval Europe* (Ithaca, N. Y.: Cornell University Press, 1978), 209.

35. Aston, "Popular Religious Movements in the Middle Ages," 170.

36. Hendrix, "In Quest of the *Vera Ecclesia*," 364–66.

37. John of Paris, *De potestate regia et papali*, ed. J. Leclercq (Paris, 1942); James of Viterbo, *De regimine Christiano*, ed. H. X. Arquilliere (Paris, 1926). Both originally appeared 1302–03.

38. Leff, "The Apostolic Ideal," 79.

39. Ibid., 67.

40. Marsilius of Padua, *Defensor pacis*, chs. 15, 16ff.

41. Quoted by Hendrix, "In Quest of the *Vera Ecclesia*," 366.

42. Karl August Fink, "The Western Schism to the Council of Pisa," in Beck, et al., *From the High Middle Ages to the Eve of the Reformation*, 424.

Notes to Chapter 2

1. Francis Oakley, "Gerson and D'Ailly: An Admonition," *Speculum* 40 (January, 1965): 74–83. Oakley makes the point that, as the situation developed, Gerson became more master than pupil.

2. Antony Black, "The Conciliar Movement," in J. H. Burns, ed., *The Cambridge History of Medieval Political Thought* (Cambridge: Cambridge University Press, 1988), 576, 580.

3. Morrall, *Gerson and the Great Schism*, 35.

4. Hans Küng, *Structures of the Church*, trans. Salvator Attanasio (Notre Dame: University of Notre Dame Press, 1968), 14. "The ecumenical council by human convocation is *really* a representation of the ecumenical council by divine convocation," 17.

5. Brian Tierney, "Conciliarism, Corporatism, and Individualism: The Doctrine of Individual Rights in Gerson," *Cristianesimo nella Storia* 9 (1988): 81–111.

6. Pascoe, *Jean Gerson: Principles of Church Reform*.

7. Morrall, *Gerson and the Great Schism*, 30. The sermon, *Adorabunt*, is found in Jean Charlier de Gerson, *Oeuvres completes*, ed. Palémon Glorieux, 7 vols. (Paris: Desclee et Cie., 1960–71), Vol. 5, document 219, pp. 28–39). Citations of Gerson's individual writings will be hereafter

identified in the text by the document number, volume, and page number(s) of this edition as follows: *Oeuvres*, d. 219, 5:28–39.

8. Glorieux, *Essai biographique*, in *Oeuvres*, d. 5, 5:108.

9. Bernard of Clairvaux, *De consideratione ad Eugenium Papam*, e.g., Bk. IV:5, in *S. Bernardi opera*, Vol. 3: *Tractatus et opuscula*, ed. Jean Leclercq and H. M. Rochais (Rome: Editiones Cistercienses, 1963).

10. Morrall, *Gerson and the Great Schism*, 30ff.

11. Ibid., 32.

12. Fink, "The Western Schism to the Council of Pisa," 410.

13. M. David Knowles, "The Great Schism," in M. David Knowles and Dimitri Obolensky, eds., *The Christian Centuries: A New History of the Catholic Church*, Vol. 2: *The Middle Ages* (New York: McGraw-Hill, 1968), 418–19.

14. Morrall, *Gerson and the Great Schism*, 38. Howard Kaminsky, *Simon de Cramaud and the Great Schism* (New Brunswick, N.J.: Rutgers University Press, 1983), 28–29, tells us that even during the lifetime of Clement the French government controlled by the dukes of Berry and Burgundy had decided to give up expansionist claims associated with Avignon, and therefore to give up the Avignon papacy as well. This switch from Avignon to work for unity was a "volte face, arguably the most important single development in international relations in the 1390s" (p. 32, quoting J. J. Palmer, *England, France, and Christendom, 1377–1399* [London, 1972]).

15. Morrall, *Gerson and the Great Schism*, 40. Kaminsky, *Simon de Cramaud*, points to a studied policy of politicizing the university on the part of the court and under the leadership of Simon de Cramaud, chief advisor to Berry, 34, 39, 48.

16. Kaminsky, *Simon de Cramaud*, 168.

17. Knowles, "The Great Schism," 419.

18. Morrall, *Gerson and the Great Schism*, 43.

Notes to Chapter 3

1. Kaminsky, *Simon de Cramaud*, 247.

2. Morrall, *Gerson and the Great Schism*, 63.

3. Kaminsky, *Simon de Cramaud*, 244; E. Delaruelle, E.-R. Labande, and Paul Ourliac, *L'Église au temps du Grand Schisme et de la crise conciliare (1378–1449)*, Vol. 14 of Augustin Fliche and Victor Martin, eds., *Histoire de l'Église depuis les origines jusqu'à nos jours* (n.c.: Bloud & Gay 1964), 103.

4. Kaminsky, *Simon de Cramaud*, 55–56.

5. Ibid., 245.

6. Morrall, *Gerson and the Great Schism*, 55–56.

7. See Walter Ullmann, *The Origins of the Great Schism* (London: Burns Oates & Washbourne Ltd., 1948), 189, who calls these conciliar views "illegal and anti-dogmatic," and Figgis, *Studies of Political Thought*

from Gerson to Grotius, 33, who thinks that the Conciliar movement was an attempt to borrow from secular legal thought and imperialist propaganda. Another who thought the conciliar thinking of Gerson imprudent, "extreme," "adventurous," and "violent" is Noël Valois, *La France et le grand schisme d'Occident*, Book IV: *Recours au Concile general* (Hildesheim: Georg Olms Verlagsbuchhandlung, 1967), 84, 290, 500.

8. Francis Oakley, "Figgis, Constance, and the Divines of Paris," *American Historical Review* 75 (1969): 368–86, points to a theological justification in Gerson's nominalism for this position: even the highest law of the Church is ordained rather than absolute power and thus is only contingent, 382–84.

9. Fink, "The Western Schism to the Council of Pisa," 414.

10. See Lambert, *Franciscan Poverty*.

11. Ibid., 143–44, 153.

12. *Cum inter nonnullos* (November 12, 1323).

13. Fink, "The Western Schism to the Council of Pisa," 413–14.

14. Morrall, *Gerson and the Great Schism*, 64. See Delaruelle, et al., *L'Église au temps du Grand Schisme*, 107–8.

15. Glorieux, "La vie et les oeuvres de Gerson," 167.

16. Morrall, *Gerson and the Great Schism*, 65.

17. Ibid., 69.

18. Delaruelle, et al., *L'Église au temps du Grand Schisme*, 121–23.

19. Morrall, *Gerson and the Great Schism*, 69; cf. Fink, "The Western Schism to the Council of Pisa," 415.

20. Morrall, *Gerson and the Great Schism*, 72.

21. Delaruelle, et al., *L'Église au temps du Grand Schisme*, 130–32.

22. Ibid.

23. Knowles, "The Great Schism," 419.

24. John A. F. Thomson, *Popes and Princes, 1417–1517: Politics and Polity in the Late Medieval Church* (London: George Allen & Unwin, 1980), xiv.

25. Morrall, *Gerson and the Great Schism*, 73–74.

26. Delaruelle, et al., *L'Église au temps du Grand Schisme*, 134.

27. For the details of the assembling at Pisa I am following the account of Delaruelle, et al., *L'Église au temps du Grand Schisme*, 136–37.

28. Morrall, *Gerson and the Great Schism*, 76. The statement needs some qualification. It would be perhaps more accurate to say that now Gerson is clear that the papacy never possesses the *ultimate* power of the Church.

Notes to Chapter 4

1. See Stanley Chodorow, *Christian Political Theory and Church Politics in the Mid-Twelfth Century: The Ecclesiology of Gratian's Decretum* (Berkeley: University of California Press, 1972).

2. Oberman has pointed out that this stricture against *vana curiositas* was characteristic of nominalist theologians in general, who were one with other reformers in wanting to purify the muddied streams of medieval theological reflection; see *The Dawn of the Reformation* (Edinburgh: T&T Clark, 1986), 208, n. 22.

3. Delaruelle, et al., *L'Église au temps du Grand Schisme*, 4:841, say that Gerson's mystical theology is nothing but an art of loving.

4. Tierney generalizes about conciliar thinkers "adapting the scriptural doctrine to their purposes by reformulating it in juridical or political language"; see "Conciliarism, Corporatism, and Individualism," 83. As was noted in chapter two above, he seems to share the assumption that the "purposes" of conciliar thinkers are based in juridical and political theory rather than in Scripture. It has been the contention here that, as concerns Gerson at least, the reverse is the case.

5. Olsen, "The Idea of the *Ecclesia primitiva*," 219; Leff, *Heresy in the Later Middle Ages*, 2; Chenu, *Nature, Man, and Society*, 252–53, 269; Ernest W. McDonnell, "The *vita apostolica* . . . ," *Church History* 24 (1955): 15; Morris, *The Papal Monarchy*, 468.

6. Tierney, "Conciliarism, Corporatism, and Individualism," 98, thinks that Gerson's concern for the claims of individual bishops and priests had as its purpose "to assert the supremacy of a general council." Quite possibly. But at least in the instance referred to above, attention to the apostolic background of Gerson's conciliarism would suggest that his primary concern was to resist the canonists' encroachments against the primacy of the preaching of the Word.

7. Tierney's remark in "Conciliarism, Corporatism, and Individualism," 98–99, 101, about the concern of Gerson's spiritual doctrine for "the individual soul's progress . . . seeking spiritual life amid the snares of the Church" properly belongs in this context, not in any justification of the supremacy of the general council.

8. G. H. M. Posthumus Meyjes, *Jean Gerson et l'assemblée de Vincennes (1329): ses conceptions de la juridiction temporelle de l'Église* (Leiden: E. J. Brill, 1978), 91.

9. Olsen, "The Idea of the *Ecclesia Primitiva*," 83, n. 59, notes that "the contrast between the austere pre-Constantinian Church and the post-Constantinian Church declining in virtue goes back to patristic times," e.g., St. Jerome, *Vita Malchi* (Migne, *Patrologia latina*, 23:55).

10. *Comm. in libr. sent.*, IV, d. 24, p. 1, a. 1, q. 3, quoted in Posthumus Meyjes, *Jean Gerson et l'assemblée de Vincennes*, 103, n. 67.

11. This was a position which the conciliarists from the outset had found necessary to develop their program. Here they were attending closely to the polemics of Ockham, which provided an arsenal of materials opposing papal jurisdictional claims against what Ockham had considered the good of the Church. E.g., *Breviloquium de principatu tyrannico*, Bk. II, ch. xxii, p. 103; ch. xxi, pp. 101–4. See Helmar

Junghans, *Ockham im Lichte der neueren Forschung*, Arbeiten zur Gescchichte und Theologie des Luthertums, 21 (Berlin & Hamburg: Lutherischs Verlagshaus, 1968), 284.

12. Reinhold Seeberg, *Textbook of the History of Doctrines*, trans. Charles E. Hay (Grand Rapids, Mich.: Baker Book House, 1898), 2:183.

13. It should obviously follow that when Gerson discusses natural law or natural rights, as he does in those passages so probingly examined by Tierney (see above, ch. 2, p. 00), he is not committing a secularist departure from his theological concern for the Church.

14. Conrad of Gelnhausen and Henry of Langenstein had introduced *epikeia* and the spirit of the legislator into conciliar discussion; see Joseph Gill, *Constance et Bâle–Florence*, Histoire des Conciles Oecumenique 9 (Paris: Editions de l'Orante, 1965), 25.

15. In the matter of the common good of the Church and *epikeia* the conciliarists closely followed the position of Ockham. See *Dialogus* III,Tr. 1, pp. 786–88. *De Imperatorum et pontificum potestate*, Bk. I, ch. viii, pp. 20–21. In general, as Tierney has pointed out in "Ockham, the Conciliar Theory and the Canonists," *Journal of the History of Ideas* 4 (1954): 49–62, the conciliarists followed Ockham where he followed the canonists. See my discussion of the prerogatives of the common good according to Ockham, John J. Ryan, *The Nature, Structure, and Function of the Church in William of Ockham*, AAR Studies in Religion 16 (Missoula, Montana: Scholars Press, 1979), 19–20.

16. The ancient tradition to this effect is represented by Gregory the Great, *Homilies*, cited in Gratian, *Decretum*, C. 11, q. 3, c. 1. St. Bernard, *Ep.* 7 n. 4 concurs. These source cited in Chodorow, *Christian Political Theory*, 117, n. 7; 115, n. 2.

17. E.g., Aquinas, *Summa theologiae*, II–IIae, 104, 5, *ad secundum*; 105, 1, *in corpore*.

18. E.g., *Contra Benedictum*, 262. See my discussion in *The Church in William of Ockham*, 10–11.

19. Yet outside of ecclesiastical circles, Oberman notes that "for over a century [i.e, before Luther] the *libertas christiana* had been a current issue and a central question in pub and marketplace" (*The Dawn of the Reformation*, 161).

20. E.g., "On the Councils and the Churches," *Works of Martin Luther*, 6 vols. (Philadelphia: United Lutheran Publication House, 1915–32), 5:270–78. There is an interesting anticipation of Luther in Gerson's description of revelation as speaking to both the "Law" and the "Gospel," *Oeuvres*, d. 271, 6:134.

21. This position, enunciated at the time of the Council of Pisa, is one example of the over-hastiness of Oberman's remark that Gerson at the opening of the Council of Constance [i.e., *not* before] had moved away from earlier attitudes and towards "ever more radical solutions." See Oberman, "The Shape of Late Medieval Thought," in *The Dawn of*

the Reformation: Essays in Late Medieval and Early Reformation Thought; Edinburgh: T&T Clark Ltd., 1986), 25. Virtually all of Gerson's "radical" positions had already been enunciated by the time of the Council of Pisa, that is, from the time he first presented himself as a convinced conciliarist.

22. Cary J. Nederman is clearly mistaken when he says that "the church does not control the office; it instead supervises the conduct of the individual incumbent of the papacy. . . . the pope whose behavior is appropriate to the office that he occupies is beyond any scrutiny; he is protected by his *plenitudo potestatis*"; see "Conciliarism and Constitutionalism: Jean Gerson and Medieval Political Thought,"*History of European Ideas* 12/2 (1990): 197. For Gerson the church's *plenitudo* is the only ultimate power. As to a pope "whose behavior is appropriate," we shall see below how Gerson can dispose of him. Also see note 31 below.

23. Paul de Vooght, *Les Pouvoirs du concile et l'autorite du pape au concile de Constance* (Paris: Les Editions du Cerf, 1965), 26, 42.

24. See Dietrich of Niem's description of Urban's torture of the aged cardinal of Venice, *De schismate*, ed. Erler, I, lii, 94, in E. F. Jacob, *Essays in the Conciliar Epoch* (Manchester: Manchester University Press, 1953), 33.

25. Tierney, *Foundations of the Conciliar Theory*, 63–64. Tierney reproduces Huguccio's crucial Gloss on the words *Nisi deprehendatur a fide devius*, Appendix I, 248–50. Huguccio of Pisa there lists "notorious robbery, notorious simony, notorious, public fornication and sacrilege" as reasons for papal deposition; as to heresy, the pope must publicly and contumaciously adhere to it before he can be judged.

26. Tierney, *Foundations of the Conciliar Theory*, 67.

27. Quoted by Gill, *Constance et Bâle–Florence*, 317, from *Opera omnia*, ed. Ellies Du Pin (Anvers, 1706), 2:273–80. It seems clear that Gerson would have regarded the contemporary dispute (Gill, de Vooght, Tierney, et al.) about the putative "infallible" (*de fide definita*) character of the Constance pronouncement as missing the point. For Gerson, the question is not one of *intent* on the part of the pronouncers. Either the pronouncement substantially embodies the "eternal Gospel," in which case it is of divine faith, or it does not.

28. Another contradiction of Oberman's remark (see note 21 above).

29. Nederman, "Conciliarism and Constitutionalism," 189–209, has arguably failed to make his case that Gerson's conciliar thinking follows the general medieval pattern, which annuls the authority of office only in case of the moral failure of the office-holder (196–98). Gerson makes it clear that even circumstances *alone* can justify the deposition of a legitimate pope.

30. Knowles, "The Great Schism," 417.

31. Fink, "The Western Schism to the Council of Pisa," 403–4.

32. Valois, *La France et le grand schisme d'Occident*, 84, calls these

"adventurous doctrines very little conformed to his earlier declarations." This strikes one as excessively complacent and insensitive to the situation.

Notes to Chapter 5

1. William of Ockham, *Dialogus*, ed. Melchior Goldast, Vol. II of *Monarchiae sancti romani imperii* (Frankfort: Conrad Riermann & Associates, 1614). See, e.g., pars I, lib. 6, p. 605; pars III, tr. 2, pp. 929–30.

2. Cited by Gill, *Constance et Bâle–Florence*, 318.

3. Tierney, "Conciliarism, Corporatism, and Individualism," 81–111, notes this departure provoked by the situation of the council, without, I think correctly tracing it to its ultimate source. He identifies the "clearly subjective definition of *jus* [right]" (85), which he thinks grows out of Gerson's spiritual doctrine and its concern for the soul's struggle for progress in the spiritual life. While this may well be the case, it is not the ultimate reason why Gerson at the Council "felt it necessary to defend the claims of individual bishops and parish priests" (98). If Gerson there is asserting "the supremacy of a general council" that supremacy has as little to do with "individual rights" as with pseudo-Dionysian hierarchical order. It is evoked rather by his primordial, communitarisn vision of the Church as the Mystical Body of Christ. Through the individual members that body speaks.

4. It is obvious that Gerson here is placing his hopes in something much more elemental than "the structural reform of Gerson" referred to by Oberman, *The Dawn of the Reformation*, 37.

5. Black, *Council and Commune*, 25, points out that in this matter the subsequent Council of Basle, following the collapse of reform, took Gerson's views "a great deal further."

6. Ozment, "The University and the Church," 124, n. 38.

7. Delaruelle, et al., *L'Église au temps du Grand Schisme*, 840; Heiko A. Oberman, "*Depuis Occam jusqu'a Luther: Ouvrages recent*," *Concilium* 17 (1966): 105–13.

8. Oakley, "Figgis, Constance, and the Divines of Paris," 379, referring to this discussion in the *De potestate ecclesiastica*, takes this position as including the laity.

9. Louis B. Pascoe, S.J., "Jean Gerson: Mysticism, Conciliarism, and Reform," *Annuarium historiae conciliorum* 6 (1974): 135–53.

10. Here and subsequently Pascoe's form of Gerson citations is followed.

11. The failure to note this presence of the apostolic concern in Gerson's understanding of the papal crisis has confused the otherwise telling question James Biechler has posed to Pascoe in his review of the latter's book, *Journal of Ecumenical Studies* 12:1 (Winter, 1975): 103. He asks: does Pascoe appreciate the "revolutionary implications of Gerson's

views regarding mystical theology and the *exalted and authoritative role the theologian plays"* in the work of reform (emphasis added)? It is not Gerson's mystical theology which is revolutionary (there Pascoe is correct) but rather his apostolic concern, which is responsible for this exaltation of the theologian's role.

12. Since this summary was written I have become aware of a newer work touching Gerson's ecclesiology, which I have not yet been able to obtain, Mark S. Burrows, *Jean Gerson and De Consolatione Theologiae (1418): The Consolation of a Biblical and Reforming Theology for a Disordered Age* (Tübingen: J. C. B. Mohr [Paul Siebeck], 1991). In a review of this work (*Journal of Ecclesiastical History* 44 [1993]: 341–42), J. H. Burns reports Burrows as emphasizing Gerson's "unswerving conservatism" in his ecclesiology and Burrows' claim that his treatment constitutes a "substantial historiographical revision." That looks to this writer like the wrong revision.

13. John B. Morrall, *Political Thought in Medieval Times* (London: Hutchinson & Co. Ltd., 1958), 128.

14. See my *The Nature, Structure, and Function of the Church in William of Ockham*.

15. Karl August Fink, "The Council of Constance," in Beck, et al., *From the High Middle Ages to the Eve of the Reformation*, 4:448–473.

16. H. Denzinger and A. Schonmetzer, S.J., *Enchiridion Symbolorum: Definitionum et Declarationum de Rebus Fidei et Morum*, 23rd editon (Freiburg Breisgau: Herder, 1965), 315–25.

17. See Knowles, "The Great Schism," 418. In the same work, after commenting that Hus had no idea of "the weight of traditional theology and canonical discipline that was still taken for granted by the prelates assembled at Constance" ("Heresy and Revolution," 454), Knowles goes on to say that in this matter [papal supremacy] "the council that condemned him could in truth throw no stones" (ibid., 455).

18. Ullmann, *Origins of the Great Schism*.

19. This assessment seems to be shared by Knowles ("The Religious Climate of the Fifteenth Century," 460), who blames the recalcitrance of the papal rivals for allowing "a conciliar doctrine to emerge into the realm of practical politics from the pages of academic discussion."

20. Knowles, "The Religious Climate of the Fifteenth Century," 460.

21. Williston Walker and D. W. Lotz, "The Reforming Councils," in Williston Walker, with Richard A. Norris, David W. Lotz, and Robert T. Handy, *A History of the Christian Church*, 4th edition (New York: Charles Scribner's Sons, 1985), 390–91.

22. Again, an honorable mention, this time on the non-Roman side, must be made for the unusually attentive and perceptive treatment of Steven Ozment, *The Age of Reform, 1250–1550* (New Haven: Yale University Press, 1980), 155–72, who has had the insight to emphasize the contribution of Gerson and who has, beyond the usual comments about

the constitutional consequences of conciliarism, clearly left open the question of the reform possibilities of conciliarism for church life.

23. To the suggestion that such ideas have already been legitimately canvassed in the documents of Vatican II, it might be retorted that the timid move toward episcopal collegiality with the pope present in the documents of Vatican II, which Rome has since effectually ignored, is hardly what the late-medieval conciliarists had in mind.

Bibliography

Aston, Margaret. "Popular Religious Movements in the Middle Ages." In Geoffrey Barraclough, ed., *The Christian World: A Social and Cultural History*. New York: Harry Abrams, Inc., 1981.

Anagnine, E. *Dolcino e il movimento ereticale all' inizio del trecento*. Florence, 1964.

Bernard of Clairvaux. *S. Bernardi opera*, Vol. 3: *Tractatus et opuscula*. Ed. Jean Leclercq and H. M. Rochais. Rome: Editiones Cistercienses, 1963.

Biechler, James. "Review of Louis B. Pascoe, S.J., *Jean Gerson: Principles of Church Reform*". *Journal of Ecumenical Studies* 12:1 (Winter, 1975): 103.

Black, Antony J. "The Conciliar Movement." In J. H. Burns, ed., *The Cambridge History of Medieval Political Thought*. Cambridge: Cambridge University Press, 1988.

―――. *Council and Commune: The Conciliar Movement and the Fifteenth Century Heritage*. London: Burns & Oates, 1979.

Brooke, Rosalind B. *The Coming of the Friars*. London: George Allen and Unwin Ltd., 1975.

Burns, J. H. "Review of Mark S. Burrows, *Jean Gerson and De Consolatione Theologiae (1418): The Consolation of a Biblical and Reforming Theology for a Disordered Age*." *Journal of Ecclesiastical History* 44 [1993]: 341–42.

Burrows, Mark S. *Jean Gerson and De Consolatione Theologiae (1418): The Consolation of a Biblical and Reforming Theology for a Disordered Age*. Tübingen: J. C. B. Mohr (Paul Siebeck), 1991.

Cameron, James K. "Conciliarism in Theory and Practice 1378–1418." Ph.D. Diss., Hartford Seminary Foundation, 1953.

Chenu, M.-D., O.P. *Nature, Man, and Society in the Twelfth Century: Essays on New Theological Perspectives in the Latin West*. Ed. and trans. Jerome Taylor and Lester K. Little. Chicago: University of Chicago Press, 1968.

Chodorow, Stanley. *Christian Political Theory and Church Politics in the Mid-Twelfth Century: The Ecclesiology of Gratian's Decretum*. Berkeley: University of California Press, 1972.

Congar, Yves M. J. *Vraie et fausse réform dans l'Église*. 2nd edition. *Unam Sanctum* 22. Paris: Editions du Cerf, 1968.

Connolly, J. L. *John Gerson, Reformer and Mystic*. Louvain: Librairie universitaire, Uystprovst, 1928.

Constable, Giles. "The Diversity of Religious Life and Acceptance of Social Pluralism in the Twelfth Century." In Derek Beales and Geoffrey Best, eds., *History, Society and the Churches: Essays in Honour of Owen Chadwick.* Cambridge: Cambridge University Press, 1985.

Delaruelle, E., E.-R. Labande, and Paul Ourliac. *L'Église au temps du Grand Schisme et de la crise conciliare (1378–1449).* Vol. 14 of Augustin Fliche and Victor Martin, eds., *Histoire de l'Église depuis les origines jusqu'à nos jours.* [Paris]: Bloud & Gay 1964.

Denzinger, H., and A. Schonmetzer, S.J., eds. *Enchiridion Symbolorum: Definitionum et Declarationum de Rebus Fidei et Morum.* 23rd editon. Freiburg Breisgau: Herder, 1965.

de Vooght, Paul. *Les Pouvoirs du concile et l'autorité du pape au concile de Constance.* Paris: Les Editions du Cerf, 1965.

Dewailly, L. M., O.P. "Notes sur l'histoire de l'adjectif 'apostolique'." *Mélanges de science religieuse* 5 (1948): 141–52.

Douie, L. D. *The Nature and the Effect of the Heresy of the Fraticelli.* Publications of the University of Manchester, Historical Series, 61. Manchester: Manchester University Press, 1932.

Figgis, J. N.. *Studies of Political Thought from Gerson to Ockham.* Cambridge: Cambridge University Press, 1931.

Fink, Karl August. "The Council of Constance." In Hans-Georg Beck, et al., *From the High Middle Ages to the Eve of the Reformation.* Trans. by Anselm Biggs. Vol. 4 of Hubert Jedin and John Dolan, eds., *The History of the Church.* New York: Seabury Press, 1980.

———. "The Western Schism to the Council of Pisa." In Hans-Georg Beck, et al., *From the High Middle Ages to the Eve of the Reformation.* Trans. by Anselm Biggs. Vol. 4 of Hubert Jedin and John Dolan, eds., *The History of the Church.* New York: Seabury Press, 1980.

Gerson, Jean Charlier de. *Oeuvres completes.* Ed. Palémon Glorieux. 7 vols. Paris: Desclee et Cie., 1960–71.

Gill, Joseph. *Constance et Bâle–Florence.* Histoire des Conciles Oecumenique 9. Paris: Editions de l'Orante, 1965.

Glorieux, P. "La vie et les oeuvres de Gerson." *Archives d'histoire doctrinale et letteraire du moyen age (1450–51)*, 149–92.

Hauck, Albert. "Die Rezeption und die Umbildung der allgemeinen Synode im Mittelalter." *Historische Vierteljahrschrift* 10 (1907): 465–82.

Heimpel, Hermann ed. *De modis uniendi et reformandi ecclesiam in concilio universali.* Leipzig-Berlin, 1953.

Hendrix, Scott W. "In Quest of the *Vera Ecclesia*: The Crisis of Late Medieval Ecclesiology." *Viator: Medieval and Renaissance Studies* 7. Berkeley: University of California Press, 1976.

Jacob, E. F. *Essays in the Conciliar Epoch.* Manchester: Manchester University Press, 1953.

James of Viterbo. *De regimine Christiano.* Ed. H. X. Arquilliere. Paris, 1926.

John of Paris. *De potestate regia et papali.* Ed. J. Leclercq. Paris, 1942.

Junghans, Helmar. *Ockham im Lichte der neueren Forschung*. Arbeiten zur Geschichte und Theologie des Luthertums, 21. Berlin & Hamburg: Lutherischs Verlagshaus, 1968..

Kaminsky, Howard. *Simon de Cramaud and the Great Schism*. New Brunswick, N.J.: Rutgers University Press, 1983.

Knowles, M. David. "The Great Schism." In M. David Knowles and Dimitri Obolensky, eds., *The Christian Centuries: A New History of the Catholic Church*, Vol. 2: *The Middle Ages*. New York: McGraw-Hill, 1968.

Küng, Hans. *The Church*. Trans. Ray and Rosaleen Ockenden. New York: Sheed and Ward, 1967.

———. *Structures of the Church*. Trans. Salvator Attanasio. Notre Dame: University of Notre Dame Press, 1968.

Ladner, Gerhart B. *The Idea of Reform: Its Impact on Christian Thought and Action in the Age of the Fathers*. Cambridge, Mass.: Harvard University Press, 1959.

Lambert, Malcolm D. *Franciscan Poverty: The Doctrine of the Absolute Poverty of Christ and the Apostles in the Franciscan Order, 1210–1323*. London: S.P.C.K., 1961.

———. *Medieval Heresy: Popular Movements from Bogomil to Hus*. New York: Holmes and Meier, 1977.

Leff, Gordon. "The Apostolic Ideal in Later Medieval Ecclesiology." *The Journal of Theological Studies*, n.s. 18 (1967): 58–82.

———. *Heresy in the Later Middle Ages: The Relation of Heterodoxy to Dissent c. 1250–1450*. Manchester: Manchester University Press, 1967.

———. "John Wyclif: The Path to Dissent." *Proceedings of the British Academy LII*, 153.

———. "What Was Conciliarism? Conciliar Theory in Historical Perspective." In Brian Tierney and Peter Lineham, eds., *Authority and Power: Studies on Medieval Law and Government*, 348–66. Cambridge: Cambridge University Press, 1980.

Little, Lester K. *Religious Poverty and the Profit Economy in Medieval Europe*. Ithaca, N. Y.: Cornell University Press, 1978.

Luther, Martin, "On the Councils and the Churches." *Works of Martin Luther*. 6 Vols. Philadelphia: United Lutheran Publication House, 1915–32. 5:270–78.

McDonnell, Ernest W. *The Beguines and Beghards in Medieval Culture*. New York: Octagon Books, 1969.

———. "The *vita apostolica*. . . ." *Church History* 24 (1955): 15.

McManners, John, ed. *The Oxford Illustrated History of Christianity*. Oxford: Oxford University Press, 1990.

Marsilius of Padua, *Defensor pacis*, chs. 15, 16ff.

Mollat, M. "La notion de la pauvreté au moyen age." *Revue d'histoire de l'Église de France* 149 (1966): 1–17.

Moorman, John. *A History of the Franciscan Order from Its Origins to the Year 1517*. Oxford: Clarendon Press, 1968.

Morrall, John B. *Gerson and the Great Schism*. Manchester: Manchester University Press, 1960.

———. *Political Thought in Medieval Times*. London: Hutchinson & Co. Ltd., 1958.

Morris, Colin. "Medieval Christendom." In Geoffrey Barraclough, ed., *The Christian World: A Social and Cultural History*. New York: Harry Abrams, Inc., 1981.

———. *The Papal Monarchy: The Western Church from 1050 to 1250*. The Oxford History of the Christian Church. Oxford: Clarendon Press, 1989.

Nederman, Cary J. "Conciliarism and Constitutionalism: Jean Gerson and Medieval Political Thought." *History of European Ideas* 12/2 (1990).

Nelson, Janet L. "Society, Theodicy, and the Origins of Heresy." *Studies in Church History* 9 (1972): 65–77.

Oakley, Francis. "Figgis, Constance, and the Divines of Paris." *American Historical Review* 75 (1969): 368–86.

———. "Gerson and D'Ailly: An Admonition." *Speculum* 40 (January, 1965): 74–83.

———. *Medieval Experience: Foundations of Western Cultural Singularity*. New York: Charles Scribner's Sons, 1974.

Oberman, Heiko A. *The Dawn of the Reformation: Essays in Late Medieval and Early Reformation Thought*. Edinburgh: T&T Clark Ltd., 1986.

———. "Depuis Occam jusqu'a Luther: Ouvrages recent." *Concilium* 17 (1966): 105–13.

———. *The Shape of Late Medieval Thought*. Edinburgh: T&T Clark, 1986.

Olsen, Glenn. "The Idea of the *Ecclesia Primitiva* in the Writings of the Twelfth Century Canonists." *Traditio* 25 (1969): 84.

Ozment, Steven. *The Age of Reform, 1250–1550*. New Haven: Yale University Press, 1980.

———. "The University and the Church: Patterns of Reform in Jean Gerson." *Medievalia et Humanistica: Studies in Medieval and Renaissance Culture*, n.s. 1 (1970): 111–26.

Palmer, J. J. *England, France, and Christendom, 1377–1399*. London, 1972).

Pascoe, Louis B. S.J. "Jean Gerson: The '*Ecclesia primitiva*' and Reform." *Traditio* 30 (1974): 379–409.

———. "Jean Gerson: Mysticism, Conciliarism, and Reform." *Annuarium historiae conciliorum* 6 (1974): 135–53.

———. *Jean Gerson: Principles of Church Reform*. Leiden: E. J. Brill, 1973.

Posthumus Meyjes, G. H. M. *Jean Gerson et l'assemblée de Vincennes (1329): ses conceptions de la juridiction temporelle de l'Église*. Leiden: E. J. Brill, 1978.

———. *Jean Gerson: zijn Kerkpolitiek en Ecclesiologie*. The Hague, 1963.

Russell, J. B. *Dissent and Reform in the Early Middle Ages*. Berkeley: University of California Press, 1965.
Ryan, John J. *The Nature, Structure, and Function of the Church in William of Ockham*. AAR Studies in Religion 16. Missoula, Montana: Scholars Press, 1979.
Salembier, L. "Gerson." In Charles G. Harbermann, ed., *The Catholic Encyclopedia*, 15 vols., 6:530–31. New York: R. Appleton Co., 1907–12.
Seeberg, Reinhold. *Textbook of the History of Doctrines*. Trans. Charles E. Hay. 2 vols. Grand Rapids, Mich.: Baker Book House, 1898.
Southern, R. W. *Western Society and the Church in the Middle Ages*. Vol. 2 of *The Pelican History of the Church*. Hammondsworth, Middlesex, England: Penguin Books, 1970.
Strauss, Gerald. *Manifestations of Discontent in Germany on the Eve of the Reformation*. Bloomington, Ind.: Indiana University Press, 1971.
Thomson, John A. F. *Popes and Princes, 1417–1517: Politics and Polity in the Late Medieval Church*. London: George Allen & Unwin, 1980.
Tierney, Brian. "Conciliarism, Corporatism, and Individualism: The Doctrine of Individual Rights in Gerson." *Cristianesimo nella Storia* 9 (1988): 81–111.
———. *Foundations of the Conciliar Theory: The Contribution of the Medieval Canonists from Gratian to the Great Schism*. Cambridge: Cambridge University Press, 1955.
———. "Ockham, the Conciliar Theory and the Canonists." *Journal of the History of Ideas* 4 (1954): 49–62.
Tocco, F. "Gli Apostolici e Fra Dolcino." *Archivio storico Italiano* 19 (1897): 241–75.
Troeltsch, Ernst. *The Social Teachings of the Christian Churches*. Trans. Olive Wyon. London: George Allen & Unwin Ltd., 1931. Harper Torchbooks edition, New York: Harper and Row, 1960.
Ullmann, Walter. *The Origins of the Great Schism*. London: Burns Oates & Washbourne Ltd., 1948.
Valois, Noël. *La France et le grand schisme d'Occident*, Book IV: *Recours au Concile general*. Hildesheim: Georg Olms Verlagsbuchhandlung, 1967.
Vauchez, André. *La Spiritualité du Moyen Age occidental: VIIIe–XIIe siècles*. Paris: Presses universitaires de France, 1975.
Walker, Williston, with Richard A. Norris, David W. Lotz, and Robert T. Handy. *A History of the Christian Church*. 4th edition. New York: Charles Scribner's Sons, 1985.
William of Ockham. *Dialogus*. Ed. Melchior Goldast. Vol. II of *Monarchiae sancti romani imperii*. Frankfort: Conrad Riermann & Associates, 1614.
Wolter, Hans. "The Crisis of the Papacy and of the Church, 1274–1303." In Hans-Georg Beck, et al., *From the High Middle Ages to the Eve of the Reformation*. Trans. by Anselm Biggs. Vol. 4 of Hubert Jedin and John Dolan, eds., *The History of the Church*. New York: Seabury Press, 1980.